BEING
ELIZABETH
BENNET

Emma Campbell Webster lives in London.
She is an actress as well as an author.
This is her first book.

BEING ELIZABETH BENNET

Create Your Own
Jane Austen Adventure

EMMA CAMPBELL WEBSTER

Atlantic Books
London

First published in Great Britain in 2007 by Atlantic Books,
an imprint of Grove Atlantic Ltd.

This paperback edition published in Great Britain in 2008 by Atlantic Books.

9 8 7 6 5 4 3 2

A CIP catalogue record for this book is available from the British Library.

ISBN: 978 1 84354 607 8

Text design: www.carrstudio.co.uk
Printed in Great Britain by CPI Bookmarque, Croydon, CR0 4TD

Atlantic Books
An imprint of Grove Atlantic Ltd
Ormond House
26–27 Boswell Street
London WC1N 3JZ

FOR MY DAD, BEN

CONTENTS

❖

YOUR MISSION

❖

*J*T IS A TRUTH universally acknowledged that a young Austen heroine must be in want of a husband, and you are no exception. Christened Elizabeth Bennet, you are tolerably beautiful, moderately accomplished, with a sharp wit and quick mind. You are the daughter of misguided but well-meaning parents and live with them and your four sisters – Jane, Mary, Kitty and Lydia – in the village of Longbourn, near the town of Meryton. You are of a happy disposition and have hitherto whiled away your years reading, walking and enjoying what limited society Meryton has to offer. A recent event however, threatens to disturb your tranquillity: a man of large fortune has let a nearby manor house. Inconsequential though this change of circumstance appears, it is the first in a long chain of events that will require you to face difficult decisions and impolite dance partners. Equipped with only your wit and natural good sense, your mission is to marry both prudently and for love, eluding undesirable suitors and avoiding family scandals which would almost certainly ruin any hope of a financially advantageous marriage for you or any of your sisters.

HOW TO PLAY

❖

*T*HIS BOOK is no ordinary book, and should not be read through from beginning to end. It contains many different adventures and the path you take will be determined by the choices you make along the way. The success (or failure!) of your mission hinges on decisions you make, so think carefully before choosing…

In addition to this, your mission will also be influenced by how well you do in the following five categories: your ACCOMPLISHMENTS, INTELLIGENCE, CONFIDENCE, CONNECTIONS and FORTUNE (which could mean either luck or money). On separate pieces of paper, draw up lists for the five different categories. You begin with high scores for your INTELLIGENCE and CONFIDENCE (200 points each) but with a regrettably low FORTUNE score (only 50 points), and absolutely no ACCOMPLISHMENTS or CONNECTIONS. In order to increase your chances of marrying well you must try to improve your scores and gain more CONNECTIONS and ACCOMPLISHMENTS. At intervals during your adventure you will be given bonus opportunities to increase your scores by taking tests or answering questions. But take care! Whilst you can gain points, you can also lose them, which could harm your chances of marrying happily and affect the outcome of your adventure.

If the mere suggestion of score-keeping gives you palpitations, fear not; you can choose not to keep track of your scores if you so wish. When asked to check them, simply choose whichever score you fancy from one of the two options you are offered.

You may now begin your adventure. Good luck!

BEING ELIZABETH BENNET

STAGE ONE

*T*HE NEWS THAT nearby Netherfield Park has been let to a man of above five thousand pounds a year greatly pleases your mother who is utterly convinced that this will immediately enhance the prospects of one or another of her daughters marrying well.

You learn from your neighbours Sir William and Lady Lucas that Mr Bingley is quite young, wonderfully handsome, extremely agreeable, and, to crown the whole, he means to be at the next assembly with a large party.

 Not a bad start. Collect 10 FORTUNE POINTS.

Nothing could be more delightful. To be fond of dancing is a certain step towards falling in love; and your mother entertains very lively hopes of one of you attaining Mr Bingley's heart. When his party enters the assembly room it consists of only five altogether – Mr Bingley, his two sisters, the husband of the eldest, and another young man.

 Hardly a 'large' party, is it? And only two of them are eligible. Mr Bingley is a disappointment already, and you haven't even met him.

Mr Bingley is good-looking and gentlemanlike; he has a pleasant countenance, and easy, unaffected manners. His sisters are fine women, with an air of decided fashion; his brother-in-law, Mr Hurst, looks the gentleman but lacks the manners and grace of one; whereas his friend Mr Darcy soon draws the attention of the room by his fine, tall person, handsome features, noble mien, and the report, which is in general circulation within five minutes after his entrance, of his having ten thousand a year.

That's more like it. Collect another 20 FORTUNE POINTS.

The gentlemen pronounce him to be a fine figure of a man, the ladies declare he is much handsomer than Mr Bingley, and he is looked at with great admiration for about half the evening till his manners give a disgust which turns the tide of his popularity. He is discovered to be proud, to be above his company, and above being pleased; and not all his large estate in Derbyshire can save him from having a most forbidding, disagreeable countenance, and being unworthy of comparison with his friend. Your own opinion of him is soon decided when, having been obliged by the scarcity of gentlemen to sit down for two dances, you are near enough to overhear a conversation between him and Mr Bingley in which Mr Bingley draws Darcy's attention to the fact that you are without a partner. Mr Darcy turns to look at you for a moment till, catching your eye, he withdraws his own and coldly says, 'She is tolerable; but not handsome enough to tempt me; and I am in no humour at present to give consequence to young ladies who are slighted by other men.'

Oh dear. You pretend not to care, but you do. Deduct 10 CONFIDENCE POINTS.

This leaves you with far from cordial feelings towards Darcy. You soon recover yourself, however, and at your first opportunity you tell your story with great spirit among your friends and family. Your mother's dislike of his general behaviour is sharpened into particular resentment by this slighting of you and she pronounces him, in characteristic hyperbole, to be the 'proudest, most disagreeable man in the world'. Her general spirits cannot be dampened, however, and when you all return home to reflect on the evening, it becomes apparent that, based on Mr Bingley having danced with Jane as many as two times throughout the course of the evening, your mother has high hopes of him shortly becoming her own son-in-law. She is particularly happy since Jane has always been her 'favourite daughter'.

Whereas you continue to be a disappointment.

A few days later, you and Jane wait on the ladies of Netherfield Park, and the visit is returned in due form. You cannot like them, though their kindness to Jane, such as it is, has some value in it since it arises in all probability from the influence of their brother's admiration. That he does admire her you are certain; and to you it is equally evident that Jane is on the way to being very much in love, though, because of her great composure, it is not likely to be discovered by the rest of the world.

Occupied as you are in observing Mr Bingley's attentions to your sister, you do not immediately notice that Mr Darcy, who recently made it clear to himself and his friends that you have hardly a good feature in your face, has begun to attend to your conversations with others. You first become aware of this new behaviour several days later when Mr Darcy approaches you and your dear friend Charlotte as you converse at a large gathering held by her father, Sir William. You are incensed by the impertinence of Darcy's intrusion.

'How dare he!' you exclaim indignantly.

Whilst you stand by and watch the dancing, you overhear Sir William endeavouring to ingratiate himself with Mr Darcy by expressing his great love of dancing. Much of the conversation passes you by, until Sir William loudly insists upon uniting you and Mr Darcy in the aforementioned activity. You are immediately alarmed. Nothing could be further from your wishes than to dance with Darcy. Furthermore, you have no desire to dance with *any* man who does not think you 'tolerable' enough to ask for the privilege himself.

 Next to your list of ACCOMPLISHMENTS, draw up a list headed 'FAILINGS'. Make sure you leave plenty of room – you're going to need it.

 Add 'Resentful' to your list of FAILINGS and deduct 10 INTELLIGENCE POINTS.

Extremely surprised though he is by Sir William's suggestion, and though it was so offensive an idea the last time it was proposed, Mr Darcy seems not unwilling to receive the presentation this time. You hastily reply with some discomposure however, that you have not the least intention of dancing. Your resistance does not appear to injure the gentleman, but before he can respond he is accosted by Miss Bingley who, to your great relief, swiftly draws him away. You go in search of Charlotte and do your best to avoid Mr Darcy.

Charlotte's friendship and conversation is invaluable to you, especially at times such as this. Divide your list of CONNECTIONS into a small column for 'SUPERIOR CONNECTIONS' and a REALLY LARGE column for 'INFERIOR CONNECTIONS'. Add 'Charlotte Lucas' to your list of SUPERIOR CONNECTIONS. Congratulations. You now have ONE SUPERIOR CONNECTION.

Mr Darcy no longer appears to listen to your conversations, but you cannot help occasionally looking in his direction and you notice that whenever your eye falls on him he seems to be just at that moment withdrawing his glance from you. You are once again enraged by his impertinence. What does he mean by always staring at you? You lead Charlotte to another part of the room where you no longer have to look at him, and the rest of the evening passes away pleasantly until the party draws to a close and you return home with the rest of your family.

The following day, Jane receives a dinner invitation from Miss Bingley and Mrs Hurst, but to your mother's disappointment it would seem that Mr Bingley is dining out on this particular evening. Your mother refuses to give Jane the carriage and insists on sending her on horseback, knowing very well that it is likely to rain and Jane will be forced to stay the night at Netherfield. You are well used to your mother's schemes by now, but endangering Jane's health solely for the purpose of promoting romance seems to you not only careless and unfeeling, but also hardly likely to achieve its end: a red nose and a sore throat have not often inspired feelings of ardour.

Your mother is so anxious to marry you all off that she may very well kill you in the process. Deduct 10 FORTUNE POINTS for having such a negligent mother.

Not long after your sister's departure, your mother's scheme is rewarded by a heavy downpour of rain, but it is not until the following morning that she is aware of the full felicity of her contrivance. A note arrives from Jane stating that she has caught a bad cold, her friends will not hear of her leaving, and they are currently awaiting the arrival of the doctor. Your anxiety for your sister's welfare is so great that you desire to visit Netherfield to assess her condition. Your mother refuses to give you either horse or carriage despite unpleasant conditions and you therefore embark on the three-mile walk to Netherfield alone.

 Luckily for both you and Jane, you have a healthy appetite for walking. Add 'Love of Walking' to your list of ACCOMPLISHMENTS.

You make your journey at a quick pace without a care for your appearance, eagerly jumping over stiles and springing over puddles, spurred on by your creditable devotion to your sister. You hastily climb over a gate and find yourself in a field you don't recognize. There are two paths ahead of you.

To take the path to the left, turn to page 19.

To take the path to the right, turn to page 30.

You stay a few days longer to ensure Jane is fully recovered. Your caution is rewarded as she takes a turn for the worse again that evening, and you are obliged to stay yet longer. Thankfully, the following day there is a change in company as a Mr Henry Crawford, his sister Mary and their friend Mr Yates arrive at Netherfield.[1] Mary Crawford is remarkably pretty, and Henry Crawford, though not handsome, has air, countenance and a fortune of five thousand pounds a year; and the manners of both are lively and pleasant. Mr Yates has not much to recommend him beyond his large estate of Mansfield Park, and a love of acting. He suggests that the Netherfield party put on a play and the Bingleys and Crawfords agree that it is a capital plan. Mr Bingley is a great fan of the theatre, and is delighted to have the chance to try a little acting himself; Miss Bingley, it appears, is a great fan of Mr Crawford, and is only too happy to join in his scheme; and Mrs Hurst refuses to be left out of anything Miss Bingley is doing. You are greatly surprised by their want of propriety; Mr Darcy protests, but in vain, and the play *Lovers' Vows* is decided upon. You are rather surprised that it has even been considered; the female characters are so unfit to be expressed by any woman of modesty that you can hardly suppose the Bingley sisters can be aware of what they are engaging in. You, at least, refuse to be drawn into such an improper scheme.

Collect 10 INTELLIGENCE POINTS.

Miss Bingley and Mrs Hurst both wish to play the tragic part of Agatha, mother of the illegitimate Frederick, who is to be played by Mr Crawford. Having been away in the army for five years, Frederick returns to find his mother begging on the street and very near death. He vows to find the wealthy father who abandoned them both before his birth. Frederick and Agatha therefore have many scenes together, and both Miss Bingley and Mrs Hurst wish to play opposite Mr Crawford. On many occasions prior to coming to Netherfield, Henry Crawford, it would seem, paid Miss Bingley attentions that have given rise to many tender feelings on her part. He paid her sister even *more*, however, and, shocking though it is, now petitions for Mrs Hurst to play the coveted part, prompting Miss Bingley to leave the room in jealous disgust. Miss Bingley now either sits in gloomy silence; or, allowing the attentions of Mr Yates, talks with forced gaiety to him alone, ridiculing the acting of the others. It seems to you that Miss Bingley's feelings for Mr Crawford surpass even those you are sure she has for Mr Darcy. Next time you are alone with Miss Crawford you share this observation with her.

'I dare say she is in love with my brother,' she replies coldly. 'I imagine both sisters are.'

'Both!' you exclaim, horrified at the idea of a married woman allowing the attentions of any man other than her husband. 'No, no, that must not be. Think of Mr Hurst.'

'You had better tell Mrs Hurst to think of Mr Hurst. It may do *her* some good.'

You have no intention of doing anything of the sort, however; Mrs Hurst has never shown you the slightest attention beyond the commonest civility, and has abused you in private when she believed you could not hear. You have no wish to involve yourself in her affairs any more than is strictly necessary. You only worry for Jane that Mr Bingley's married sister should so discredit her brother by encouraging and reciprocating Mr Crawford's flirtation.

That evening the happy actors realize they are missing a Cottager's Wife and suddenly petition you to take the role.

'Me!' you cry in great surprise. 'Indeed you must excuse me. I could not act anything if you were to give me the world. No, indeed, I cannot act.'

 There is nothing more immoral than a woman on the stage. Collect 10 INTELLIGENCE POINTS for your superior sense of decorum.

'Phoo! Phoo!' replies Mrs Hurst. 'Do not be so shamefaced. Every allowance will be made for you. We do not expect perfection. You must get a brown gown, and a white apron, and a mob cap, and we must make you a few wrinkles, and a little of the crowsfoot at the corner of your eyes, and you will be a very proper, little old woman.'

'You must excuse me,' you insist, thinking how insupportable it would be to act in a production with those for whom you have such low regard, 'indeed you must.'

'Do not urge her, madam,' interrupts Mr Darcy. 'It is not fair to urge her in this manner. You see she does not like to act. Let her choose for herself, as well as the rest of us. Do not urge her any more.'

You are quite taken by surprise at this show of gallantry from Mr Darcy, and know not what to make of it.

 This is a rare compliment from Darcy. Such unlooked for attention raises your CONFIDENCE whether you like it or not. Collect 10 bonus CONFIDENCE POINTS.

The role of Cottager's Wife is cut from the play, and rehearsals commence the next day. You watch as you work and see with concern that Mr Crawford continues to pay his attentions to Mrs Hurst. You are very glad that Jane is not present to witness Bingley's sister indulging the flirtation. Perhaps fearing that his behaviour is giving rise to hopes that he has no intentions of fulfilling, however, on the third day of rehearsals Mr Crawford has an apparent change of heart and redirects his attention away from Mrs Hurst and towards you, endeavouring, it would seem, to make you in love with him. Your contempt for him only increases and you are determined not to be taken in by his charms.

Over the next fortnight, however, Mr Crawford pays you such gallant attention that you begin to feel that he might be in love with you after all. Astonishing though it is, it really seems to be true. There is something in his eyes when he speaks to you that seems to communicate something beyond his words and he presses your hand with such meaning that you cannot help but soften your resolve against him. You can hardly believe yourself. You fight against it as best you can, but Mr Crawford seems sincerely to love you and you cannot resist his affections forever. However disingenuous he was when he first paid his attentions to you it seems as if, almost against his better judgement, he has genuinely fallen in love with you and is now entirely serious in his intentions. He seems to understand that you value good sense above all else and each day modifies his behaviour so that it is so different from what it has been, so far improved that when Jane is well enough to join you all downstairs once again, even *she* begins to wish you in love with him.

Your heart and mind are in tumult; you are wary of his fickle heart, but cannot remain immune to such devotion. At the end of his third week at Netherfield, Mr Crawford makes a formal declaration.

To give in to your overwhelming impulses and accept Mr Crawford, trusting in his change of character and the security of his five thousand a year, turn to page 50.

To refuse him, wary of his sudden change in character, turn to page 54.

An unfortunate accident in Derbyshire however, sees the end of your hopes when, on one particularly stormy night, your carriage overturns. Mr W (as you affectionately call him)[2] is flung from the vehicle and crushed to death when its full weight falls upon him.

You begin to think of returning to your father and mother but give over the design when you learn that they too have been tragically killed in an accident incurred while in pursuit of you. Bereft of all else, and though there is nothing more immoral than a woman on the stage, your only hope is to forsake decorum and engage yourself to some strolling company of players, despite never having acted in your life before. You offer your services to one and are accepted. Your company is indeed rather small as it consists only of the manager, his wife, the driver of the carriage which crushed Mr W to death, and you; but there are fewer to pay and the only inconvenience attending it is the scarcity of plays which, for want of people to fill the characters, you are able to perform. You do not mind trifles, however. One of your most admired performances is *Macbeth*, in which you are truly great. The manager always plays Banquo himself; his wife Lady Macbeth. You do the three witches, and the carriage driver acts all the rest. To say the truth, this tragedy is not only the best, but the *only* play you ever perform, and after having acted it all over England and Wales you go to Scotland to exhibit it over the remainder of Great Britain.

When you finally tire of *Macbeth*, you take up residence in a romantic village in the Highlands of Scotland where you can, uninterrupted by unmeaning visits, indulge in a melancholy solitude, your unceasing lamentations for the death of your father, mother and fiancé.

You are never again in the society of men, and despite your early success on the stage, end your days in poverty and obscurity.

THE END

Clearly, you have failed.

100 *OR ABOVE*

You accept the colonel's offer and you both return to Hertfordshire to be married at the earliest opportunity. Your marriage is happy at first, but it soon becomes apparent that your temperaments are not that well matched: it would appear Colonel Brandon underestimated your confidence and independence of spirit. As a result, you often argue over matters of little consequence. Though you try to deal with the problem by spending as much time as possible in the company of others, your husband finds your confidence and independence threatening and puts you down in front of your friends and family. It really gets you down.

You remain married, but not particularly happily.

THE END

You might have married for love, but the love has DIED.

This marriage is a failure, and so are you.

The following morning your mother, accompanied by your younger sisters Kitty and Lydia, visits Netherfield Park with the stated intention of forming her own judgement of Jane's situation. Upon Miss Bingley's invitation, you all attend her into the breakfast parlour – which your mother finds exceptionally charming.

'I do not know a place in the country equal to Netherfield, Mr Bingley,' says she. 'You will not think of quitting it in a hurry I hope, though you have but a short lease.'

You hope that Mr Bingley does not catch her full meaning.

'Whatever I do is done in a hurry,' says Mr Bingley, 'and therefore if I should resolve to quit Netherfield, I should probably be off in five minutes. At present, however, I consider myself quite fixed here.'

'That is exactly what I should have supposed of you,' you say, having noted a similar tendency towards precipitance in his behaviour in the short time you've known him.

'I did not know before,' cries Bingley, 'that you were a studier of character. It must be an amusing study!'

'Indeed it is,' you think to yourself, 'especially with such subjects as Mr Darcy and Miss Bingley to divert me.'

'The country,' says Darcy, surprising you all by voluntarily joining in the conversation, 'can in general supply but few subjects for such a study. In a country neighbourhood you move in a very confined and unvarying society.'

You are amused by his simplistic view of country life.

'But people themselves alter so much,' you correct him, 'that there is something new to be observed in them forever.'

Mr Darcy makes no reply.

Putting Darcy right in front of his friends is surprisingly satisfying. Collect 20 CONFIDENCE POINTS.

'Yes, indeed!' interrupts your mother, clearly offended by his manner of mentioning a country neighbourhood. 'I assure you there is quite as much of that going on in the country as in town. I cannot see that London has any great advantage over the country for my part. The country is a vast deal pleasanter, is not it, Mr Bingley? But that gentleman,' she says, looking at Darcy, 'seems to think the country is nothing at all.'

You are mortified by her rudeness.

'Indeed, Mama, you are mistaken,' you say, blushing for your mother. 'You quite mistook Mr Darcy. He only meant that there are not such a variety of people to be met with in the country as in town, which you must acknowledge to be true.'

'Certainly, my dear, nobody said there were; but as to not meeting with many people in this neighbourhood, I believe there are few neighbourhoods larger. I know we dine with four and twenty families.'

Your mother's ostentatious tone only exposes her to further ridicule, and adds to your shame.

With a mother as dim as yours, it's a miracle you have any sense at all. Give yourself 10 bonus INTELLIGENCE POINTS.

Bingley thankfully keeps his countenance, but his sister is less delicate, and you catch her directing her eye towards Mr Darcy with a very expressive smile. The general pause which ensues makes you tremble lest your mother should expose herself again. You long to speak, and thereby prevent *her* from doing so, but can think of nothing to say. When your mother finally calls for the carriage, Lydia puts herself forward to tax Mr Bingley with having promised on his first coming into the country to give a ball at Netherfield. Though she is only fifteen, she is already bold and self-assured. Bingley assures her that he will keep his engagement when Jane is recovered. Lydia declares herself satisfied and she, Kitty and your mother all depart. You are relieved to see them gone, and are eager to leave the room yourself as quickly as possible. You return instantly to Jane, leaving your own and your relations' behaviour to be, you are sure, condemned by the two ladies and Mr Darcy.

 You are looking forward to Bingley's promised ball, but fear that your inferior dance skills could harm your chances of landing a rich husband. For a chance to learn a new dance, answer the following question:

How many couples face each other

when dancing a reel?

Is it

a) Two or *b) Six*

If you think the answer is a), turn to page 56.

If you think the answer is b), turn to page 43.

'THE SENSIBLE TYPE'

You are totally devoid of sensibility. When you should have been reading novels, you were probably reading sermons. Your emotions are not likely to be discovered by anybody: you conceal them so well you are barely sensible of them yourself. You are the type most likely to end up an old maid.

 Add 'The Sensible Type' to your list of FAILINGS and deduct 300 INTELLIGENCE POINTS. That ought to redress the balance a bit.

Continue on page 44.

After about half a mile you make a sudden turn into a path deeply shaded by elms on each side. You have advanced some way when you suddenly perceive at a small distance before you, a party of gypsies. A child on the watch comes towards you to beg, causing you to let out a great scream. How the vagrants might have behaved had you been more courageous is doubtful, but such an invitation for attack cannot be resisted. You are soon assailed by half a dozen children, headed by a stout woman and a thickset boy. Growing more and more frightened, you promise them money and, taking out your purse, give them a shilling, begging them not to want more, or to use you ill. You are then able to walk forwards, though slowly, and you move away from the group – but your fear and your purse are too tempting, and you are followed, or rather surrounded, by the whole gang, demanding more. When you confess that you have none, they set about attacking you until your face is so disfigured that you are never again able to attract a husband all your livelong life.[3]

THE END

That didn't take you long, did it? You have failed to complete your mission. You didn't even get NEAR completing it, in fact. You deserve to be disfigured. Be ashamed.

The next day passes much as the day before. In the evening you join the rest of the party in the drawing room.

While Mrs Hurst sings with her sister you cannot help observing once again how frequently Mr Darcy's eyes are fixed on you. Again, you are vexed by the impertinence of it. That he should look at you because he dislikes you is very strange indeed, and yet you hardly know how to suppose that you could be an object of admiration to so great a man. What can he mean by it? You decide, at last, that you draw his notice because there is something about you more wrong and reprehensible, according to his ideas of right, than in any other person present.

 It's highly likely. You do have more than one failure of perfect symmetry in your form and are wearing unfashionably long sleeves.

The supposition does not pain you however; you like him too little to care for his approbation.

After playing some Italian songs on the pianoforte, Miss Bingley varies the charm by a lively Scotch air; and soon afterwards Mr Darcy, drawing near you, says to you, 'Do not you feel a great inclination, Miss Bennet, to seize such an opportunity of dancing a reel?'

You smile, but make no answer. If he wants to insult you he may, but you will not give him the satisfaction of rising to such an inducement. He repeats the question, with some surprise at your silence and, really riled by him this time, you reply with affected gaiety, 'Oh! I heard you before; but I cannot immediately determine what to say in reply. You wanted me, I know, to say "Yes," that you might have the pleasure of despising my taste; but I always delight in overthrowing those kind of schemes, and cheating a person of their premeditated contempt. I have therefore made up my mind to tell you that I do not want to dance a reel at all – and now despise me if you dare.'

'Indeed I do not dare.'

Having rather expected to affront him, you are amazed at his gallantry. You wonder that he can bring himself to be so gallant to one whom he considered barely 'tolerable' at first sight, and whose connections must leave a great deal to be desired. You can only conclude that he does not yet know the full extent of your family's shortcomings – that you have an uncle who lives in Cheapside and another who is an attorney in Meryton.

 Your connections, it is true, are woefully inferior and this is seriously harming your chances of finding a good husband. For the chance to win a much-needed SUPERIOR CONNECTION, answer the following question:

Which is more shameful?

a) A relative living in Gracechurch Street

or

b) A relative living in Grosvenor Street

If you think the answer is a), turn to page 35.

If you think the answer is b), turn to page 41.

'THE SENSE-IBILITY TYPE'

You have some sensibility, but a little too much sense for your own good. You should be ashamed to rise from your bed not in more need of repose than when you lay down in it. You are the type most likely to make a prudent but thoroughly loveless match.

 Add 'The Sense-ibility Type' to your list of FAILINGS.

Continue on page 44.

Correct.

 Congratulations! You can now speak fluent French. Add this to your list of ACCOMPLISHMENTS.

This has increased your chances of marrying well tenfold.

 Add 'Screen-Covering Skills' to your list of ACCOMPLISHMENTS as well.

Continue on page 15.

Jane is soon so much recovered that she is able to leave her room for a couple of hours in the evening. Mr Bingley sits by her and scarcely talks to anyone else. At work in the opposite corner, you observe his tender attentions with great delight. Mr Darcy sits reading a book and Miss Bingley is perpetually either making some enquiry as to his progress, or looking at his page. You wonder that he can bear it so calmly, for he merely answers her question, and reads on. She is unable to win him to any conversation, and at last gets up and walks about the room. Her figure is elegant, and she walks well; but Darcy, at whom her display is obviously aimed, is still inflexibly studious. To your great surprise, Miss Bingley suddenly turns to you and says, 'Miss Eliza Bennet, let me persuade you to follow my example, and take a turn about the room. I assure you it is very refreshing after sitting so long in one attitude.'

Given what you overheard her saying about you on your first evening at Netherfield, such civil attention from Miss Bingley is a shock indeed. Surprised though you are however, you agree to it immediately out of sheer curiosity. Mr Darcy now looks up and is invited by Miss Bingley to join your party. To be taking a turn with Miss Bingley is strange enough, but being obliged to make conversation with Mr Darcy at the same time might be more than you can bear.

 Deduct 10 INTELLIGENCE POINTS for ever standing up with Miss Bingley in the first place.

To your great and immediate relief, he declines the invitation, saying, 'You either choose this method of passing the evening because you are in each other's confidence, and have secret affairs to discuss, or because you are conscious that your figures appear to the greatest advantage in walking.'

You cannot quite determine if there is playfulness in his meaning, or if he is being serious.

'Oh! Shocking!' cries Miss Bingley. 'I never heard anything so abominable. How shall we punish him for such a speech?'

You think for a moment and then suggest to Miss Bingley that you tease him. Intimate as she is with Darcy she must know how it is to be done. But she declares that her intimacy has not yet taught her how to do *that*.

'And as to laughter,' she concludes, 'we will not expose ourselves by attempting to laugh without a subject. Mr Darcy is beyond reproach.'

'If that is her true opinion,' you think to yourself, 'Miss Bingley really *must* be in love with him.'

Out loud you cry, 'Mr Darcy is not to be laughed at? That is an uncommon advantage and a great shame, since I dearly love a laugh.'

'Miss Bingley,' says Darcy, 'has given me credit for more than can be. The wisest and the best of men may be rendered ridiculous by a person whose first object in life is a joke.'

Mr Darcy means to defend himself using his extremely resilient Shield of Pride. You must now attempt to pierce it with your wit and intelligence.

'I hope I never ridicule what is wise or good,' you reply, choosing your words carefully. 'Follies and nonsense, whims and inconsistencies do divert me, I own. But these, I suppose, are precisely what you are without.'

25

You invite him to admit his failings by appearing to compliment him. It's a tactical approach, and a surprisingly good one. For you.

 'Perhaps that is not possible for anyone. But it has been the study of my life to avoid those weaknesses which often expose men to ridicule.'

'Such as vanity and pride,' you venture.

 Going straight for his Pride is a startlingly unsubtle move.

'Yes, vanity is a weakness indeed,' he retorts. 'But pride – where there is a real superiority of mind, pride will be always under good regulation.'

His arrogant vision of himself amuses you and you turn away to hide a smile.

 Darcy's Shield of Pride is too powerful for you this time. There will be other opportunities for attack; for now you concede defeat.

'Well,' you say to Miss Bingley, 'I am perfectly convinced now that Mr Darcy has no defect.'

'I have made no such pretension,' says Darcy with haste. 'I have faults enough. My temper I dare not vouch for – it is I believe too little yielding. I cannot forget the follies and vices of others so soon as I ought, nor their offences against myself. My good opinion once lost is lost forever.'

The idea of a person being so knowingly resentful is abhorrent to you and your already low opinion of him falls yet lower.

'That is a failing indeed!' you cry. 'But you have chosen your fault well. I really cannot laugh at it; you are safe from me.'

You consider the conversation closed and are just on the point of moving away to another part of the room when Mr Darcy adds, 'There is, I believe, in every disposition a tendency to some particular evil, a natural defect, which not even the best education can overcome.'

'And your defect,' you say with meaning, 'is a propensity to hate everybody.'

'And yours,' he replies with a smile, 'is wilfully to misunderstand them.'

 He's got a point. Deduct 10 INTELLIGENCE POINTS for wilfully misunderstanding Mr Darcy and everybody else you meet to whom you do not take an immediate shine.

Obviously tired of a conversation in which she has no share, Miss Bingley cries, 'Do let us have a little music!'

The pianoforte is opened, Miss Bingley sits down to play, and the rest of the evening passes away with no further encounters with Darcy's pride.

You are anxious to return home but are unsure whether Jane is well enough recovered for the journey. She appears to be in good health, but you know she would never admit to needing to stay longer if she felt it would be an inconvenience to anyone.

To trust in her improved appearance and urge Jane to borrow Mr Bingley's carriage immediately, turn to page 42.

To suggest Jane takes advantage of the restorative properties of fresh air and exercise by walking back the way you came, turn to page 37.

To stay a few days longer to ensure Jane is fully recovered, turn to page 7. You wouldn't want her to permanently damage her health, would you? That could harm her chances with Mr Bingley, and you stand to gain from such an advantageous match as well, remember.

'The Sentimental Type'

You have no sense of reason whatsoever, and let your heart govern all your decisions. A triumph of Sensibility! You are the type most likely to marry for love.

 Add 'The Sentimental Type' to your list of Accomplishments *and collect 50 bonus* Fortune points.

With such a high level of Sensibility you are in danger of making an astonishingly imprudent match, however.

Oh well, you can't have it all.

Continue on page 44.

The path leads you to the top of the field from where you can clearly see the way to Netherfield. You quicken your pace a little and arrive at the house with weary ankles, dirty stockings, and a face glowing with the warmth of exercise. You feel alive and refreshed and are eager to see Jane. You are shown into the breakfast parlour, where all but Jane are assembled – and where your appearance creates a great deal of surprise. That you should have walked three miles, in such dirty weather, without a care for your state of dress, and by yourself, appears almost incredible to Miss Bingley and Mrs Hurst and they clearly hold you in contempt for it.

Strike 'Love of Walking' from your list of ACCOMPLISHMENTS and add it to your list of FAILINGS.

Mr Darcy says very little, and Mr Hurst nothing at all. You are sure Mr Darcy thinks ill of you for coming so far alone, but care not what he thinks. You care even less for Mr Hurst's opinion, and in any case, from his vacant expression it seems likely that he is probably only thinking of his breakfast.

You are taken to your sister immediately; and you are both delighted to see one another. The doctor has advised Jane that she must remain in bed to get the better of her violent cold, but you are relieved to see she is in no real danger and when the clock strikes three you feel you must return home. Miss Bingley offers you the use of the carriage but when Jane testifies concern over your parting, Miss Bingley is obliged to extend an invitation to remain at Netherfield for the present, which you accept. You hope Jane's illness will not be a long-lasting one.

At dinner that night the sisters enquire after Jane, repeat three or four times how much they are grieved, how shocking it is to have a bad cold, and how excessively they dislike being ill themselves; and then think no more of the matter. Their indifference towards Jane when she is not immediately before them restores you to the enjoyment of all your original dislike.

You feel better immediately. Collect 10 CONFIDENCE POINTS.

When dinner is over, you return directly to your sister. When you have the comfort of seeing her asleep, your sense of propriety compels you to go downstairs and join your hosts, despite your inclinations to the contrary. Just as you are about to open the drawing-room door, you catch your name being used in a conversation between Miss Bingley and Mrs Hurst. You pause outside for a moment, not wishing to cause any embarrassment by interrupting them. You cannot help overhearing what they have to say about you, and it gives you no very great pleasure. Your manners are pronounced to be very bad indeed, a mixture of pride and impertinence; you have no conversation, no style, no taste, no beauty.

Ouch. Add 'No Style, Taste or Beauty' to your list of FAILINGS.

You cannot help but smart at such abuse of your character, but since you have no respect for their opinion, and had gathered they thought as much of you previously, you do not take it to heart. Mr Bingley, at least, defends your character and your affection for him can only grow as a result; you cannot blame him for his sisters. You take a moment to recover your composure, and when they have quite finished, you enter the room with renewed and vigorous feelings of antipathy towards Mr Bingley's sisters, and take a seat at the furthest possible distance from them. You politely decline the party's invitation to play a hand of whist, and much to the disgust of Mr Hurst, choose rather to read a book.

Your intellectual superiority is clear. Collect 20 INTELLIGENCE *POINTS.*

You are soon so distracted by their conversation, however, that you must leave your book wholly aside.

Then again, perhaps not. Deduct 10 INTELLIGENCE POINTS.

Miss Bingley is making enquiries after Mr Darcy's sister Georgiana, and praising her many accomplishments.

'I wonder how all young ladies find the patience to be so accomplished!' cries Mr Bingley. 'As I think they all *are.* They all paint tables, cover screens, and net purses. I am sure I never heard a young lady spoken of for the first time, without being informed that she is very accomplished.'

You have painted tables and netted purses, but never in your life have you covered a screen. You wonder with some amusement what Mr Bingley would think of you if he knew.

'Your list of the common extent of accomplishments,' says Darcy to his friend, 'has too much truth. The word is applied to many a woman who deserves it no otherwise than by netting a purse, or covering a screen. But I am very far from agreeing with you in your estimation of ladies in general. I cannot boast of knowing more than half a dozen, in the whole range of my acquaintance, that are really accomplished.'

That Mr Darcy's standards should be higher than Bingley's is nothing less than you expected. You are just beginning to wonder what it would take to satisfy Mr Darcy's expectations of a woman when Miss Bingley joins the debate and gives you some idea of it by exclaiming:

'Oh certainly, Mr Darcy! No one can be really esteemed accomplished who does not greatly surpass what is usually met with. A woman must have a thorough knowledge of music, singing, drawing, dancing, and the modern languages, to deserve the word; and besides all this, she must possess a certain something in her air and manner of walking, the tone of her voice, her address and expressions, or the word will be but half deserved.'

It is all you can do to refrain from laughing out loud at this picture of perfection. Such women may exist in London but you have certainly never met with one in Hertfordshire. From the expressive and pointed manner in which she speaks, you begin to suspect that Miss Bingley has feelings for Darcy beyond those of mere cordiality.

'All this she must possess,' adds Darcy, 'and to all this she must yet add something more substantial, in the improvement of her mind by extensive reading.'

You are no longer surprised at his only knowing six accomplished women, and rather wonder now at his knowing any. No wonder he didn't think you adequate enough to dance with.

 Your own list of ACCOMPLISHMENTS is wanting, to say the least. For the chance to gain a new one, answer the question below and follow the instructions to find out what you have learnt!

What exactly does 'covering a screen' mean?

Is it

*a) Decorating the canvas of a screen
with intricate paintings*

or

*b) Decorating the canvas of a screen
with embroidery or stitching*

If you think the answer is a), turn to page 64.

If you think the answer is b), turn to page 23.

Quite right.

Congratulations! You know that Gracechurch Street is in Cheapside, a most unfashionable part of London and therefore to be avoided at all costs. Mr Darcy may perhaps have heard of such a place, but he would hardly think a month's ablution enough to cleanse him from its impurities, were he once to enter it.[4]

 Add 'A Distant Cousin Living in Grosvenor Street' to your list of SUPERIOR CONNECTIONS. This has marginally improved your chances of marrying well but there is still a LONG way to go.

Continue on page 24.

BELOW 100

You accept the colonel's offer and you both return to Hertfordshire to be married at the earliest opportunity. You find yourself submitting to new attachments, entering on new duties, placed in a new home, a wife, mistress of a family, and the patroness of a village. Your own happiness is perhaps surpassed only by Colonel Brandon's, and your mother, always having preferred Jane to you, is for once inclined to think you her favourite for being the first of her daughters to marry, and for marrying so well.

THE END

> *Congratulations.*
>
> *You have completed your mission.*

You set off early the next morning and deliver Jane safely to the garden gate. You are enjoying the freedom of a walk in the open air so much that you decide to go on alone. You continue past your house and gaily ascend the hills before you, catching in your face the animating gales of a high south-westerly wind. Suddenly the clouds unite over your head, and a driving rain sets full in your face. You turn back, running with all possible speed down the steep side of the hill which leads immediately to your garden gate, but a false step brings you suddenly to the ground. A gentleman carrying a gun happens to be passing up the hill and within a few yards of you when your accident happens and runs to your assistance. Your foot has been twisted in the fall and you are scarcely able to stand. The gentleman offers his services, and perceiving that your modesty declines what your situation renders necessary, takes you up in his arms without further delay and carries you down the hill. He bears you directly into the house and quits not his hold till he has seated you in a chair in the parlour.

Your mother and sisters rise up in amazement at your entrance, and the eyes of all are fixed on him with an evident wonder and, you are sure, a secret admiration. He apologizes for his intrusion by relating its cause in a manner so frank and so graceful that his person, which is uncommonly handsome, receives additional charms from his voice and expression. Your mother thanks him again and again; and invites him to be seated, but this he declines for fear of leaving a water mark. She then begs to know to whom she is obliged. His name, he replies, is Willoughby, his estate Combe Magna in Somersetshire and his present home is at Meryton with his cousin Mrs Smith, from whence he hopes your mother will allow him the honour of calling tomorrow to enquire after you.

The attentions of such a man instantly swells your CONFIDENCE; collect 20 CONFIDENCE POINTS!

The honour is readily granted, and he then departs, to make himself still more interesting, in the midst of a heavy rain, with no regard for what havoc it might wreak on his health – or his coat. You mother declares him more handsome even than Mr Bingley, and her rapturous delight at making his acquaintance is surpassed only by your own.

Wanting to know Willoughby's pursuits, his talents, his genius, you petition Sir William for information when he pays you all an afternoon visit. Sir William knows everyone in the neighbourhood and you are sure he will be able to tell you all you wish to know about the stranger. Your hopes of learning more are disappointed, however, and you discover only that Willoughby is a pleasant, good-humoured fellow, who has the nicest black bitch of a pointer Sir William has ever seen. You are disgusted by Sir William's lack of sensibility, and determine in future to consult only your instincts when assessing character. Your instincts tell you to think well of Willoughby.

Your instincts are unreliable. Deduct 50 INTELLIGENCE POINTS for being so stupidly naive.

You earnestly hope that Willoughby will honour his promise to visit you in the morning and you are not disappointed: early the next day he calls to enquire after your health. You receive him with great pleasure and he converses with you for many hours. You feel as if you have known each other for a lifetime, and his fondness for Cowper's poetry is second only to his love of Shakespeare's sonnets in the innumerable list of his merits. As your ankle's swelling subsides your affection grows, and soon your quiet neighbourhood is disturbed by your riotous and imprudent jaunts in his carriage.

Love has robbed you of your characteristic good sense and, unable to see or think of the world beyond your intimate sphere of two, you throw caution and prudence to the wind. Jane cautions you against such unrestrained behaviour but you are so very much in love that you disregard her advice, believing that where the heart leads, no wrong can follow. Willoughby begs a lock of hair from you and taking up your scissors cuts off a long one, kisses it and folds it up in a piece of white paper and puts it into his pocketbook.

You and your family are certain that it will not be long until the two of you are united in marriage, and one Sunday you stay behind from church to facilitate the anticipated proposal. No sooner have your mother and sisters entered the house on their return, however, than you come out of the parlour with your handkerchief at your eyes, and without looking at them, run up the stairs. Willoughby has just told you that Mrs Smith has exercised the privilege of riches upon a poor dependent cousin, by sending Willoughby on business to London. He has no intention of returning to Meryton.[5]

This latest disappointment will be a great test of your sensibility. Your reaction must exactly match the level of your distress. Take the following **Sensibility Test** and see which Sensibility Type you are.

The man you love, and from whom you were expecting a proposal of marriage, suddenly leaves the countryside with no immediate plans to return.

Do you

a) *Try your hardest to conceal your emotions from your family for fear of giving them any share of the pain that you feel all too strongly yourself.*

b) *Take your place at dinner that night with eyes red and swollen, restraining your tears with difficulty, neither eating nor speaking; but awake the next morning with a greater degree of composure following a reasonable night's sleep.*

c) *Take your place at dinner that night with eyes red and swollen, restraining your tears with difficulty, neither eating nor speaking; then rise from your bed the next morning more in need of repose than when you lay down in it, unable to talk, unwilling to take any nourishment and giving pain every moment to your family.*

If you answered a), turn to page 18.

If you answered b), turn to page 22.

If you answered c), turn to page 29.

Wrong.

Oh dear. How could you not know that Grosvenor Street is a highly fashionable residential area of London just south of Oxford Street, while Gracechurch Street is in Cheapside? Cheap by name, cheap by nature, Gracechurch Street is in one of London's least fashionable areas.

Deduct 100 INTELLIGENCE POINTS.

Your chances of marrying well have been seriously compromised.

Continue on page 24.

41

You urge Jane to borrow Mr Bingley's carriage immediately and the communication excites so many professions of concern for Jane that your going is deferred till the morrow. To Mr Darcy you imagine your departure is welcome intelligence; he scarcely speaks ten words to you through the whole of Saturday, and though you are at one time left by yourselves for half an hour, he adheres most conscientiously to his book, and will not even look at you. On Sunday you take leave of the whole party in the liveliest spirits.

Congratulations! You have completed Stage One.

You remain miserably poor, unconnected and talentless. Remember Miss Bingley's list of accomplishments? You've got a long way to go before you'll be fit to attract a husband of any real worth, rich or otherwise.

Proceed to Stage Two on page 67.

You are quite wrong.

 Only two couples face each other when dancing a reel. Failure to grasp even the basics of country dancing proves you to be more coarse than even Miss Bingley first surmised. Add 'Insufficient Knowledge of Dancing' to your list of FAILINGS.

Continue on page 20.

Following Willoughby's removal from Hertfordshire, your melancholy and your family's concern continue uninterrupted until you are invited to London by your friend Charlotte's parents, Sir William and Lady Lucas. Though it must mean being away from Mr Bingley at this important stage of their courtship, Jane generously agrees to accompany you. The prospect of seeing Willoughby again brightens your spirits immeasurably, and you feel that all will soon be put to rights.

Your departure takes place in the first week in January and you arrive three days later, glad to be released, after such a journey, from the confinement of a carriage, and ready to enjoy all the luxury of a good fire. As dinner is not to be ready in less than two hours from your arrival, you determine to employ the interval in writing to Willoughby.

You can scarcely eat any dinner, and when you afterwards return to the drawing room you anxiously listen to the sound of every carriage. A loud rap is suddenly heard which cannot be mistaken for one at any other house and, expecting Willoughby, you start up and move towards the door. Everything is silent; and the suspense is overwhelming. It is to your great disappointment then, that Sir William's friend Colonel Brandon appears. The colonel has become a friend to you and Jane on his frequent visits to Sir William back in Longbourn and long since has been a great admirer of yours. His face is not unpleasing and though he is on the wrong side of five and thirty his countenance is sensible and his address is particularly gentlemanlike. Though you acknowledge him to be a good man, you feel nothing above common regard for him and since you cannot return them, his attentions are therefore not altogether welcome.

His appearance at this moment is too great a disappointment to be borne with calmness, and you immediately leave the room.

 The colonel has done nothing to deserve such a reception. Add 'Insensitive Rudeness' to your FAILINGS.

Colonel Brandon has a general invitation to the house and in the following days calls on you often. Knowing, as she does, your devotion to Willoughby, Jane tells you that she is concerned by Brandon's apparently strengthening regard for you, but you disregard her worries.

About a week after your arrival you find Willoughby's card on the table when you come in from the morning's drive. Your heart leaps, and you are dearly disappointed that you missed him. You insist on being left behind the next morning when the others go out, but Willoughby does not return.

 Your CONFIDENCE is plummeting. Deduct 20 points.

The following day you learn from Jane that Colonel Brandon has visited. She tells you that he had asked her, in a voice of some agitation, when he was to congratulate her on the acquisition of a brother. It seems that others have been talking of your engagement to Willoughby as a certainty. This only increases your feeling of distress: you alone know that no formal engagement has been entered into. From what she tells you, it seems that Jane led Colonel Brandon to believe that you and Willoughby *are* engaged, and though she does not press you, you know that she is waiting for confirmation from you as to whether or not it is true. You remain silent, however, reluctant to admit that you are not, and still clinging to the hope that you will very soon be so. Jane finishes by relating to you with concern Colonel Brandon's parting words: 'To your sister I wish all imaginable happiness; to Willoughby that he may endeavour to deserve her.'

'What do you think he could have meant by it?' Jane asks with evident concern.

She is worried that the colonel might know something about Willoughby's character that has been hidden from you, but you pay no attention to her concerns. It seems only to you the natural sentiment of a man disappointed in love, and you immediately turn your thoughts back to Willoughby, and your anxiety over when he will come to you.

<hr />

During the next four days Willoughby neither comes nor writes.

 Deduct 10 CONFIDENCE POINTS.

You are engaged to attend Lady Lucas to a party, for which, wholly dispirited, careless of your appearance, and seeming equally indifferent whether you go or stay, you prepare without one look of hope or one expression of pleasure.

You arrive in due time at the place of destination, and when you have paid your tribute of politeness by curtsying to the lady of the house, you are permitted to mingle in the crowd. You sit down close to the card table but do not remain in this manner long before you perceive Willoughby standing within a few yards of you, in earnest conversation with a very fashionable-looking young woman. With a countenance glowing with sudden delight, you go to move towards him but Jane instantly catches hold of you.

'Why does he not look at me?' you whisper to Jane, your anxiety growing with every passing moment.

'Pray, be composed,' urges Jane. 'Perhaps he has not observed you yet.'

This, however, you know is more than she can believe herself. Such trying circumstances rob you of your reason, and you cannot calm your agitated nerves however hard you try. You sit down at last, but your impatience affects every feature.

At last he turns round again, and regards you both; you start up, and hold out your hand to him. He approaches, and addressing himself rather to Jane than you, as if wishing to avoid your eye and determined not to observe your attitude, enquires in a hurried manner after your mother and asks how long you have been in town. His cold civility is so cruel a shock that you do not immediately know what to say in reply. Your face crimsons over, and you exclaim in a voice of uncharacteristic emotion, 'Good God! Willoughby, what is the meaning of this? Have you not received my letters? Will you not shake hands with me?'

He cannot then avoid the act, but your touch seems painful to him, and he holds your hand only for a moment. You try everything in your power to contain your distress and Willoughby too appears to be struggling for composure. After a moment's pause, he speaks with calmness.

'I did myself the honour of calling in Berkeley Street last Tuesday, and very much regretted that I was not fortunate enough to find yourselves and Lady Lucas at home. My card was not lost, I hope.'

A thousand feelings rush upon you at once, and try as you might, you cannot hide your suffering.

'But have you not received my notes?' you cry, before taking hold of yourself and continuing in a lower voice. 'Here is some mistake, I am sure – some dreadful mistake. What can be the meaning of it? Tell me, Willoughby, what is the matter?'

He makes no reply; his complexion changes and all his embarrassment returns; but as if, on catching the eye of the young lady with whom he had been previously talking, he feels the necessity of instant exertion, he recovers himself again and after saying, 'Yes, I had the pleasure of receiving the information of your arrival in town, which you were so good as to send me,' turns hastily away with a slight bow and joins his friend.

 Your CONFIDENCE is nose-diving. Deduct 50 points.

Never could you have imagined that one once so passionate could be so unfeeling towards you, and your wretchedness is beyond measure. Shock, above all else, overwhelms you. Looking dreadfully white you sink into your chair, and Jane, expecting every moment to see you faint, tries to screen you from the observation of others, for which you are grateful.

In a short time Jane sees Willoughby quit the room by the door towards the staircase, and telling you that he is gone, urges the impossibility of speaking to him again that evening as a fresh argument for you to be calm. You are torn between an earnest wish to follow him and a sense of propriety which must forbid it.

To ignore your better judgement and follow Willoughby out of the room to confront him and the lady directly, turn to page 65.

To comply with your sister's entreaties and wait until the morning when you hope to be more reasonable, turn to page 52.

Difficult though it is, you give up Colonel Brandon and return home to Longbourn with your father and Jane at the earliest opportunity. You never see the colonel again and Sir William never speaks of him to you.

You turn your thoughts to Netherfield and you hope that your extended departure has not harmed your sister's chances with Mr Bingley. You visit Netherfield the day following your return and find Mr Bingley as attentive to Jane as he ever was; Miss Bingley as unpleasant as she was wont to be; and Mr Darcy as taciturn and proud as you imagine he has been his entire life. You slip back into life at Longbourn with such ease that it soon feels as if you were never away.

Congratulations! You have completed Stage One.

You remain miserably poor, unconnected and talentless however, so don't get too excited. If you're hoping to attract a better offer than the colonel's, you're going to have to try a LOT harder.

Proceed to Stage Two on page 67.

You accept Mr Crawford and are wed soon afterwards. You have not been married long, however, before he elopes with Mrs Hurst, breaking your heart and involving you in a most terrible scandal. This ruins the chances of any of your sisters marrying well and you are all forced to work as governesses.[6]

THE END

You have failed to complete your mission.

THE SENTIMENTAL TYPE

Directly after reading it you attempt to rise from the bed. Jane enters just in time to prevent you from falling on the floor, faint and giddy from a long want of proper rest and food; for it is many days since you have had an appetite, and many nights since you have really slept; and now, when your mind is no longer supported by the fever of suspense, the consequence of all this is felt in an aching head, a weakened stomach, and a general nervous faintness. Jane immediately procures for you a glass of wine. Seated at the foot of the bed, with your head leaning against one of its posts, you once again take up Willoughby's letter, and after shuddering over every sentence, exclaim, 'It is too much! Cruel, cruel Willoughby – nothing can acquit you now. "The lock of hair" (repeating it from the letter), "which you so obligingly bestowed upon me" – that is unpardonable. Willoughby, where was your heart when you wrote those words? Oh! Barbarously insolent!'

 You are a complete wreck. Well done! Collect 50 bonus FORTUNE POINTS.

 Your CONFIDENCE *is at an all-time low. Deduct 200 points.*

Continue on page 57.

You are too miserable to stay a minute longer and instantly beg Jane to entreat Lady Lucas to take you home.

Before the housemaid has lit your fire the next day, you write to Willoughby by what little light your window affords. As breakfast is a favourite meal with Lady Lucas, it lasts a considerable time, and all the while you think of Willoughby. Just as you finish eating, a letter in a familiar hand is delivered to you which you eagerly catch from the servant. Reading its contents you are shocked to the core. You feel yourself turning pale and growing faint, and you instantly run out of the room. Jane quickly follows you and finds you stretched on the bed, overcome by tears of grief, the most recent letter in your hand, and others lying by you. Though unable to speak you put all the letters into Jane's hands and she reads the most recent first. He is sorry, she reads, if there was anything in his behaviour last night that did not meet your approbation and is at a loss to discover in what point he could be so unfortunate as to offend you. His esteem for your whole family is very sincere, but if he has been so unfortunate as to give rise to a belief of more than he felt, or meant to express, he shall reproach himself for not having been more guarded in his professions of that esteem. He finishes his letter by informing you that he is engaged to be married to another, and obeys your commands by returning all your letters, and the lock of hair which you 'so obligingly bestowed' on him.

Jane's feelings on reading such a letter can be well imagined.

To see how YOU reacted to reading it, turn to the appropriate page for your Sensibility Type.

If you are The Sensible Type, turn to page 66.

If you are The Sense-ibility Type, turn to page 63.

If you are The Sentimental Type, turn to page 51.

—————◦◦◦◦————

You politely refuse Mr Crawford, but though you doubted him, it turns out that he has truly fallen in love with you. Unwilling to admit defeat readily, he secretly visits your father, and you are first made aware of this by the prompt arrival of your mother at Netherfield. Almost without introduction, she begins her abuse. 'You are a foolish, headstrong girl Lizzy! The advantage or disadvantage of your family, of your parents, your sisters, never seems to have had a moment's share in your thoughts. How *they* might be benefited, how *they* must rejoice in such an establishment for you, is nothing to *you*. Oh, no! You think only of yourself, and because you do not feel for Mr Crawford exactly what a young heated fancy imagines to be necessary for happiness, you resolve to refuse him at once, and are, in a wild fit of folly, throwing away from you such an opportunity of being settled in life as will probably never occur to you again!'

You feel the blood rising in your cheeks. Though you acknowledge the truth of what she says about your obligation to your family, her abuse of your character does not please you. Far from acting in a 'wild fit of folly', you have given it your deepest consideration.

'I am sorry to give you pain, Mama,' you reply with as much composure as possible, 'but nothing you could say would induce me to accept a man I do not love. Mr Crawford's affections have but lately been directed towards me, and I am sure he will soon learn to redirect them towards another without material difficulty and will not therefore suffer too greatly from his present loss.'

Your mother takes leave of you in an agitation even angrier than the one in which she arrived.

Though he really loved you, Mr Crawford is not one given to reflection and does not pine for you long. He leaves Netherfield for London and it is not long before you hear a scandalous report of him. Not content with unsettling Mrs Hurst's marriage, Mr Crawford has seduced and eloped with a married woman of society and is living with her in sin and shame, outcast from his family and all polite society. You are glad you refused him, and return home with Jane, leaving the Bingleys to recover from their friend's scandal.

Well done. You have completed Stage One.

You remain miserably poor, unconnected and talentless however, so don't get too excited. Remember Miss Bingley's list of accomplishments? You've got a long way to go before you'll be fit to attract a husband of any real worth.

Proceed to Stage Two on page 67.

Correct.

> *Congratulations! You learn the Boulanger, a dance requiring little skill, derived from an eighteenth-century cotillion figure and made up of a circle of couples who have the pleasure of swapping partners until they have danced at least once with every member of the opposite sex.[7] Add this to your list of* ACCOMPLISHMENTS!

This won't have any effect whatsoever on your chances of marrying well.

Continue on page 20.

Jane then reads the other letters you have written to Willoughby since arriving in London. Her condemnation of him does not blind her to the impropriety of their having been written at all, full as they are of such affection and confidence. It is an impropriety you are well aware of.

'I felt myself,' you argue in your defence, 'to be as solemnly engaged to him, as if the strictest legal covenant had bound us to each other.'

 This was clearly a stupid assumption. Deduct 10 INTELLIGENCE POINTS.

You long to go home, but are obliged to stay in London and fulfil your engagement with Lady Lucas. Two weeks after receiving Willoughby's letter you hear the news that he is married. Though you knew it must happen, you had until this moment held out hope that Willoughby would somehow yet be yours. This news confirms it all; Willoughby is entirely lost to you, and the pain you feel at hearing it is not soon to be forgotten. You bear it with outward composure, however, though for the remaining weeks of your stay in London you take little interest in your appearance or the daily activities you must endure.

You are really letting yourself go. This will significantly lower your chances of attracting other men, especially the rich ones. Deduct 50 INTELLIGENCE POINTS.

You have now been rather more than two months in town, and your impatience to be gone increases every day. Fortunately,

Lady Lucas is to visit her niece at Cleveland about the end of March for the Easter holidays and you receive a very warm invitation from her to go too. This must take you into the very county where you had once looked forward to going, but which you now dread seeing, the county where Willoughby lives, but you have little choice: though it is some distance out of your way, Lady Lucas has offered you her carriage to take you home afterwards and *that* is an offer you can't refuse. Jane too is eager to return home, and though she will never admit it, you are sure that a desire to be once more in the company of Mr Bingley is her chief inducement.

Your journey to Cleveland is safely performed and after three days' drive you enter the house with nerves greatly agitated from the consciousness of being not thirty miles from Combe Magna. Two sombre twilight walks on the third and fourth evenings of your being there in the most distant parts of the grounds, where the grass is the longest and wettest – assisted by the still greater imprudence of sitting in your wet shoes and stockings – give you an extremely violent cold.

 Well, what a surprise. Deduct 20 INTELLIGENCE POINTS for wilfully endangering your health.

The doctor is sent for, who pronounces your disorder to have a putrid tendency. Lady Lucas determines very early in the seizure that you will never get over it, and Colonel Brandon, recently arrived from London with Sir William, cannot expel from his mind the persuasion that he shall see you no more. Your repose becomes more and more disturbed; Jane perceives with alarm that you are not quite yourself; your pulse is lower and quicker than ever; and you talk so wildly of 'Papa' that Colonel Brandon offers to fetch him and departs immediately.

You remain in a heavy stupor for a number of days and are therefore unaware of the extraordinary event that happens during that time. It is not until you are sufficiently recovered, and your father and Colonel Brandon are safely arrived, that Jane tells you the story of what happened. You are sitting with Jane by the fire one evening, when you mention Willoughby's name fondly in conversation. Perhaps fearing a renewal of your affection for him, Jane decides to tell you the following story of what happened when you were ill.

On the fourth day of your illness, the doctor had declared you entirely out of danger. On hearing a carriage drive up to the house Jane assumed it to herald the arrival of your father and the colonel. She rushed towards the drawing room, entered it, and to her great surprise, saw only Willoughby. He had heard you were dying, and was greatly relieved therefore to hear that you were out of danger.

It seems he doesn't entirely hate you after all. Your CONFIDENCE *is a little revived. Collect 10 points.*

Immediately regretting having come, he then resolved to make it not a wasted journey by offering to Jane some explanation, some kind of apology for the past. Jane was unsure of how to react to such improper candidness, but felt at last that even Willoughby must be given a chance to defend himself, if such a thing were at all possible.

'He determined to pay his addresses to you,' says Jane, 'but, unwilling to enter into an engagement while his financial circumstances were so greatly embarrassed, put off the moment of doing so.'

Again, his intentions were apparently honourable. Collect a further 20 CONFIDENCE POINTS.

'Before he could confirm his affections to you,' Jane continues, 'an unlucky circumstance occurred. Mrs Smith was informed of a scandal involving Willoughby and an orphan in the care of Colonel Brandon by the name of Eliza. It was Sir William who was able to give Jane the full details of his friend Brandon's tragic story. Willoughby met, seduced, and eloped with Eliza when she was fourteen and staying at Bath with a friend.'

Your CONFIDENCE instantly collapses again. Deduct 50 CONFIDENCE POINTS.

It was not until eight months later that Brandon could discover Eliza's whereabouts, by which time Willoughby had left her, never to return, in a situation of the utmost distress and heavy with child. Willoughby's character – expensive, dissipated, and worse than both – is now before you. A thousand feelings rush upon you at once.

He's worse than you ever could have imagined. Deduct a further 50 CONFIDENCE POINTS.

That you could have been so deceived in Willoughby is painful enough, but you have until this moment been unable to banish all your feelings of affection for him. This news, however, must kill them all.

'When Mrs Smith discovered this scandal,' Jane continues, 'Willoughby was dismissed from her favour and went to London with a "heavy heart" and thinking only of you. The unfeeling letter you received from him the day following the ball where you met was in fact composed by Miss Grey whose fortune was the only thing that attracted Willoughby to her. In his own words, Lizzy, he "sacrificed his *and* your feelings to vanity and avarice to avoid a comparative poverty which your affection and society would have deprived of all its horrors". By raising himself to affluence he lost everything that could make it a blessing.'

 Add 'Ability to be Happy in Reduced Circumstances' to your ACCOMPLISHMENTS. You'll need it at this rate.

It is some time before you can fully recover from this story, though you betray nothing of your discomposure to Jane. Though you know it shouldn't be, it is of some comfort to know that Willoughby still loves you. It is hard for you to forget the Willoughby you knew that summer in Hertfordshire, but for his dishonourable and disgraceful behaviour towards Eliza, you can never forgive him.

Over the next few days, your teasing father leads you to believe that Colonel Brandon has confessed his love for you. In the light of Jane's story, your feelings towards him are not as hard as they once were and over time you come to think of him with some degree of fondness. After diligently reading you Shakespeare's sonnets through the long weeks of your recovery, Colonel Brandon makes you an offer of marriage.

If you wish to accept the kind, loving and wealthy colonel, you must first check your CONFIDENCE SCORE.

If it is 100 or above, turn to page 14.

If it is below 100, turn to page 36.

If, on the other hand, you feel that there might be a better match for you out there, you can refuse his offer and continue your search on page 49.

THE SENSE-IBILITY TYPE

You read it with indignation. Though aware, before you began it, that it must bring a confession of his inconstancy, and confirm your separation forever, you were not aware that such language could be suffered to announce it. You cry for some minutes, but a glass of wine that Jane procures directly for you makes you more comfortable. You allow yourself to be consoled by Jane's sensible advice and know that such grief must have its course.

 Your reaction is hardly sufficient for the circumstances. Deduct 100 INTELLIGENCE POINTS and try harder next time.

Continue on page 57.

Wrong.

Oh dear. Covering a screen means decorating the canvas of a screen with embroidery or stitching. How could you not know that? Your ignorance is astounding.

 Add 'Insufficient Knowledge of Embroidery' to your list of FAILINGS.

This has seriously compromised your chances of attracting a rich husband.

Continue on page 15.

Ignoring Jane's pleas to wait till the morning, you immediately quit the room in search of Willoughby. You step out in the street and are greeted by a scene of great confusion and commotion. In their hurry to be gone, Willoughby and the fashionable Miss Grey, to whom you later discover he was engaged, neglected to take sufficient care when crossing the street and the young lady was tragically run down by a passing carriage. You run to Willoughby who, always having loved you and now freed from his engagement to Miss Grey, hires the very carriage which lately ran down one fiancée to carry you, her timely replacement, to Gretna Green.

 This is an uncharacteristically stupid thing to do. Deduct 20 INTELLIGENCE POINTS.

Continue on page 12.

THE SENSIBLE TYPE

You read it with indignation. Though aware, before you began it, that it must bring a confession of his inconstancy, and confirm your separation forever, you were not aware that such language could be suffered to announce it. You hide the depth of your emotion from Jane in order to spare her any share of the pain you feel all too deeply yourself.

 A shockingly inadequate reaction; deduct 100 FORTUNE POINTS.

Continue on page 57.

STAGE TWO

*S*HORTLY AFTER your return, your father announces that he is expecting an addition to your family party. About a month ago he received a letter from your cousin Mr Collins who, since your family estate is entailed away, may turn you all out of your house as soon as he pleases when your father is dead. Your mother cannot bear to hear that odious man's name mentioned, but is a little softened by some of what Mr Collins has to say:

He has been so fortunate as to be distinguished by the patronage of the Right Honourable Lady Catherine de Bourgh, widow of Sir Lewis de Bourgh, whose bounty and beneficence has preferred him to the valuable rectory of the parish of Hunsford in Kent. He begs leave to apologize for being next in the entail of Longbourn estate and being the means of injuring Mr Bennet's amiable daughters, and assures your father of his readiness to make those daughters every possible amends.

You can only guess that he means by marrying one of you.

 At least you'd be saved from homelessness. Collect 10 bonus FORTUNE POINTS.

Your father confesses to you great hopes of finding him ridiculous and there is a mixture of servility and self-importance in his letter which promises well. Mr Collins is punctual to his time and is received with great politeness by the whole family. He is a tall, heavy-looking young man of five and twenty. His air is grave and stately, and his manners are extremely formal. During dinner Mr Collins launches into a panegyric on his patroness Lady Catherine de Bourgh and her sickly daughter Anne, towards whom he conceives himself peculiarly bound to pay little attentions which he admits to often rehearsing.

You'd rather be homeless than married to Mr Collins. Deduct 10 FORTUNE POINTS.

It soon becomes clear that you were right: Mr Collins means to choose one of you for a wife to make amends for inheriting your father's estate. You sincerely hope he does not choose you as his means of doing so, but are no less concerned when you see that it is Jane's lovely face that quickly captures his attention. You mention it to your mother who soon cautions him against her. Far from being disheartened, Mr Collins simply redirects his attentions towards you instead, seemingly without a second thought. You wish you had kept quiet.

———————

The following morning you, your sisters and Mr Collins walk to Meryton to visit your aunt Philips. A small militia regiment has recently taken residence at Meryton, and your sisters are always keen to get the latest news on the officers from your obliging aunt. As you enter Meryton, your attention is soon caught by a young man of most gentlemanlike appearance walking on the other side of the way with Mr Denny, an officer with whom you have become acquainted at your aunt Philips's. Mr Denny entreats permission to introduce his friend, Mr Wickham, who has accepted a commission in Denny's corps. His appearance is greatly in his favour; he has all the best part of beauty – a fine countenance, a good figure, and very pleasing address. You like him immediately.

 Collect 10 bonus FORTUNE POINTS.

You are all standing and talking together very agreeably when the sound of horses draws your notice, and Darcy and Bingley come riding down the street directly towards you. They are just beginning the usual civilities when Mr Darcy's eyes are suddenly arrested by the sight of the stranger and, happening to see the countenance of both as they look at each other, you are all astonishment at the effect of the meeting. Both change colour, one looks white, the other red. Mr Wickham, after a few moments, touches his hat – a salutation which Mr Darcy just deigns to return.

 This is an extraordinary and significant exchange and nobody but you has noticed it. Add 'Highly Observant' to your list of ACCOMPLISHMENTS.

It is impossible to imagine what could be the meaning of it; it is impossible not to long to know.

 Add 'Incredibly Nosy' to your list of FAILINGS.

In another minute Mr Bingley, without seeming to have noticed what just passed, takes leave and rides on with his friend. Mr Denny and Mr Wickham accompany you to the door of Mr Philips's house, and then make their bows.

Your aunt promises to invite Mr Wickham to a dinner she has planned for some of the other officers tomorrow night. The prospect of such delights is very cheering, and you part in mutual good spirits. As you walk home, you relate to Jane what you saw pass between Wickham and Darcy; but unfortunately Jane can no more explain such behaviour than you.

The following day, your coach conveys you all at a suitable hour to Meryton. When Mr Wickham walks into the room, you feel that he is far beyond the other officers in person, countenance, air, and walk. He is the happy man towards whom almost every female eye turns, and you are the happy woman by whom he finally seats himself.

 Your vanity is gratified. Collect 30 CONFIDENCE POINTS.

 Vanity is a sin. Deduct 20 FORTUNE POINTS.

The card tables are placed, and while the others play at whist, Mr Wickham talks to you. You are longing to ask the history of his acquaintance with Mr Darcy, but delicacy forbids you.

To observe discretion, daring not to even mention that gentleman to him, turn to page 116.

To ask anyway, turn to page 98.

To prevent him continuing his odious proposal one minute longer you hastily interject and accept his offer. His delight is great, and he professes himself to be the happiest man alive.

'Lady Catherine will, I'm sure, find you as delightful as I; have no fear on that point my dear Elizabeth!'

Mrs Bennet bursts into the room to offer her congratulations, and following her come Mary, Kitty and Lydia. You leave them to the attentions of Mr Collins, and go in search of Jane. Her shock at your news is great, which only pains you further. After she has had some moments to recover, she begins to see all the benefits of the situation, and encourages you to do the same.

'You have saved your sisters and mother, Lizzy,' says she. 'Think how grateful your whole family will be. You shall have all the pleasure of passing your adult years in familiar surroundings, with all your fondest recollections of the past to cheer you, and at a close distance to your oldest friends and family. And Hunsford, I'm sure, will have much to recommend it in the meantime.'

You listen in silence, looking out of the window. She is trying to comfort you, but Jane's representation of your future seems bleak to you; it seems but a future spent thinking of the past. You survey the view and consider what a price has been paid to keep Longbourn within the family.

In the early afternoon your father calls you to his library.

'My dearest Lizzy,' says your father, 'pray comfort me. A most horrible joke has been played upon you. Your mother and sisters would have me believe that you are to be married to our cousin Mr Collins. Had it not been for Mr Collins's venturing so far as to apologize for the inconvenience that removing you from your family home might cause, I would not have wasted your time by calling you here. All this can be settled in a moment: tell me that you are not to marry Mr Collins.'

Your father's certainty that it cannot be true only serves to increase your shame and misery.

'Father, I cannot. Mr Collins has proposed to me, and I have accepted him.'

Mr Bennet is silent. His face colours to a deep crimson, and then to the palest white. With a grave expression he finally speaks these words to you: 'I offer you my deepest sympathy. To this I will only add my advice: that your greatest chance of happiness lies in creating for yourself a library as soon as is possible after your arrival at Hunsford.'

You can only nod in reply.

'Very well, Lizzy, you may go.'

You leave the library in even heavier spirits than those in which you entered it.

Your wedding is a mercifully modest and quiet affair, with only your nearest friends and relatives present to witness the sealing of your unhappy fate. With many tears on your mother's side, and not a few on your own, your family sees you off in your carriage on the way to Hunsford, and certain wretchedness. You arrive at the parsonage in good time, and make the most of the remaining light by taking a walk in the garden you are to call yours until the unhappy day your father dies. You catch a glimpse of Rosings Park between the trees and wonder how many painful hours will be passed there in the ensuing months.

Time passes slowly. You endeavour to continue 'expanding your mind through extensive reading', remembering the words of Mr Darcy on female accomplishments, and your father's advice on your best chance of happiness.

Give yourself 50 INTELLIGENCE POINTS (for all the good it'll do you now).

You write frequently to Charlotte and your family, but their replies are not as swift as you would have hoped. You are at pains to find enough employment to fill your days, and you take longer and longer walks so as to be spared the torment of conversation with your husband. You wonder how long you can continue in the present situation. You return home from your walk to a barrage of mindless talk from your husband. To call it conversation would be to do a disservice to the talents of Mr Collins who is able to talk so ceaselessly without the need of an interlocutor as to render the term 'conversation' redundant. In vain do you seek a corner of the house in which he is out of hearing; no matter where you hide, he finds you.

And so it goes on, day after day, until you can bear it no longer. Having rejected all thoughts of suicide, you consider rendering yourself deaf to be your greatest chance of comfort. One day, when Mr Collins is spending the morning at Rosings consulting Lady Catherine over some proposed alterations to your garden path, you go to his room in search of a medical text that will explain how to perform this miracle. In increasing distress do you tear volume upon volume from the shelf in search of one that might give some hint as to how this injury might best be affected without incurring any further damage to your faculties. The time approaches when your husband must surely return and still you have found nothing. With a cry of desperate panic do you greet the sound of Lady Catherine's carriage delivering him home. In a matter of moments the sound of his feet will be heard approaching you through the hall, shortly to be followed by the intolerable, unbearable, insufferable, torturous blabberings of the man himself. You tear at the pages of the volume in your hand, distracted and unhinged in your inexorable suffering. Before you know it his hand is on the door handle.

'My dearest Elizabeth, once again Lady Catherine has honoured us with her condescension and has suggested that we move the garden path seven degrees to the…'

He thrusts open the door just in time to see you, *Fordyce's Sermons* in hand and raised aloft, high above your head.

'My dear Elizabeth!'

'No more!' you cry, and with that you hurl *Fordyce's Sermons* directly at his head, killing him in an instant.[8]

It is some moments before you regain your composure and come to a full realization of the events that have just passed. Swiftly following on from your immediate feelings of guilt and horror comes the pleasant realization that you are now free to return to Longbourn, and since there is no male heir left to whom the estate can be entailed away, you can only assume that it will remain with your own dear family. You wonder why you didn't think of it before, and begin to devise a way of making his death appear natural.

THE END

Delighted though you are, this marriage was neither happy nor equal and you are now the cause of what will become a devastating family scandal that will prevent any of your sisters from ever engaging in a financially advantageous marriage. This might not be such an issue now that the Longbourn estate is returned to your family, but your sisters can never forgive you and you can never again show your face in polite society.

You have FAILED.

You dance in silence, vexed to be opposite the man to whom you fancy you owe all the evening's disappointment. Wickham is uppermost in your thoughts, and your mind once more goes over his many grievances as you dance. Your disgust for Mr Darcy is so great that it is all you can do to prevent yourself from 'accidentally' stepping on his toes. The look of hauteur which never leaves his features only sharpens all your feelings of disdain into outright repugnance, and you cannot wait to be released from him. As soon as the dance is over, you step outside to get some air and regain your composure. It is unusually cold for the time of year but you find the chill refreshing. You take a short walk around the house and admire the grounds, which appear to uncommon advantage in the bright moonlight. It really is cold and, fearing for your health, you turn back and head in the direction of the ballroom. In your haste to be once again in the warmth of the ballroom you break into a run and, not taking care to watch your step, slip on some ice and break your neck.

The End

> ## *YOU FAIL!*
>
> *Who ever said life was fair?*

'His pride has often led him to be liberal and generous,' explains Wickham, 'to give his money freely, to display hospitality, to assist his tenants, and relieve the poor. Family pride, and *filial* pride, for he is very proud of what his father was, have done this. He has also *brotherly* pride, which with *some* brotherly affection, makes him a very kind and careful guardian of his sister.'

You find it hard to believe and regard this favourable account of Darcy as proof merely of Mr Wickham's admirable generosity of character.

 Deduct 10 INTELLIGENCE POINTS for continuing in your Wilful Prejudice.

Miss Darcy he describes as 'too much like her brother – very, very proud'.

You are extremely pleased to have your opinion of Mr Darcy confirmed by Mr Wickham, and it appears to you, indeed, that on almost everything the two of you discuss, your thoughts and opinions are as one. You cannot but smile when you think on it, and your attachment to Wickham increases with every pleasing reflection.

 Add 'Mr Wickham' to your list of SUPERIOR CONNECTIONS.

Mr Wickham's attention is suddenly caught when he overhears Mr Collins talking of his patroness Lady Catherine de Bourgh. Wickham informs you that Lady Catherine and Darcy's mother, Lady Anne Darcy, are sisters; Lady Catherine's daughter Miss de Bourgh will have a very large fortune and it is believed that she and her cousin Mr Darcy will unite the two estates. This information makes you smile as you think of poor Miss Bingley. Vain indeed must be all her attentions to Darcy if he is already self-destined to another.

You go away that night with your head full of Mr Wickham and relate his story to Jane the next day. She listens with astonishment and concern; she cannot believe either of them to be in the wrong, and determines therefore to continue to think well of them both. You cannot agree with her on this point and can easily believe Mr Darcy to be in the wrong. You tease her for her inability to think ill of anyone, no matter how incriminating the evidence against them might be.

The two of you are summoned from your conversation by the arrival of some of the very persons of whom you have been speaking; Mr Bingley and his sisters have come to Longbourn to give their personal invitation for the long-expected ball at Netherfield.

You think with pleasure of dancing a great deal with Mr Wickham and your spirits are so high that, though you do not often speak unnecessarily to Mr Collins, you cannot help asking him whether, as a clergyman, he intends to accept Mr Bingley's invitation. You are rather surprised to find that he entertains no scruple whatever with regard to that matter and he immediately solicits your hand for the first two dances. You feel completely taken in; you had fully proposed being engaged by Wickham for those very dances – and to have Mr Collins instead! Your liveliness has never been worse timed.

 Add 'Poorly Timed Liveliness' to your extensive list of Failings.

There is no help for it, however. Mr Wickham's happiness and your own is perforce delayed a little longer, and Mr Collins's proposal accepted with as good a grace as you can manage.

Till you enter the drawing room at Netherfield and look in vain for Mr Wickham among the cluster of red coats there assembled, a doubt of his being present never occurs to you. Mr Denny tells you that Wickham has been obliged to go to town on business and is not yet returned; adding, with a significant smile, 'I do not imagine his business would have called him away just now, if he had not wished to avoid a certain gentleman here.'

Every feeling of displeasure against Darcy that this summons in you is sharpened by immediate disappointment and you can barely reply with tolerable civility to the polite enquiries that Mr Darcy soon approaches to make. The first two dances bring more distress. Mr Collins, awkward and solemn, apologizing instead of attending, and often moving wrongly without being aware of it, gives you all the shame and misery which a disagreeable partner for a couple of dances can give.

 Deduct 10 Confidence points.

The moment of your release from him is ecstasy.

You return to Charlotte Lucas, and are in conversation with her, when you find yourself suddenly addressed by Mr Darcy, who takes you so much by surprise in his application for your hand that you are at a loss for some moments as to what to say.

To accept his application, conscious of the very great dignity to which you will be raised by standing opposite so great a man, turn to page 133.

To reject his application, and remain faithful in your loyalties to the amiable Mr Wickham, turn to page 135.

⸺⸺≫◆≪⸺⸺

You wait patiently for a convenient time for Miss Tilney to accompany you, but three days pass without her making mention of her promise, and you begin to think that she must have forgotten it. You are on your way to remind her of it when you pass the door to the library. You know it is the general's favourite room, and conscious that you might find some clues therein, you cannot resist taking a look.

You really are astoundingly nosy. Deduct 20 INTELLIGENCE POINTS for flagrantly overstepping every boundary of decorum.

You enter the library and find it a handsome room of generous proportions, lined with shelves of books. Your attention is soon drawn to a set of books on a shelf next to the fireplace. They are bound in dark blue leather with gilt lettering, so small you cannot make out the titles. You go to examine one in greater detail, and when you pull the book from the shelf, to your great surprise, a secret doorway opens in the wall. Your heart pounds with excitement and though you are scared, you cannot resist the temptation to see where the door will lead.

Nosy, nosy, nosy.

Taking a last look around to be sure that you have not been observed, you slip through the door and carefully close it behind you.

You find yourself in a long dark corridor, and setting off boldly, you soon come to a set of stone steps spiralling upwards into the darkness. Your pulse quickens. Determined to continue, you climb the steps until you grow so tired, so sure that they will never lead anywhere, that you begin to fear for your safety. You are sure that you will be missed below by Miss Tilney, and how are you to explain your absence? You wish Mr Tilney had never introduced you to gothic literature.

You only have yourself to blame. Deduct 10 INTELLIGENCE POINTS for blaming Mr Tilney.

Finally, you reach the top of the stairs, and come face to face with a large wooden door. Never one to forget your manners, you politely knock three times then draw back to wait and see if anyone, or anything, will open the door to you. After a few moments, you hear noises from within, and then a gentle voice calls out 'Come in'. You boldly step forward and open the door.

Inside you are surprised to see a white attic of good proportions.[9] You had rather expected to find a gloomy cell.

Sitting at a small writing desk before you is a young girl of about eighteen years, with a slight frame and plain features. You are extremely confused as to where you are, and who this girl could be. You have never heard Henry or Eleanor talk of another relative living in the abbey, and she seems too well dressed to be a servant. The girl's eyes brighten at the sight of you and you suspect it has been some time since anyone last came by this way.

'Hello,' she says.

'Hello,' you reply, hesitantly.

She does not immediately say anything else, and so after a few moments, feeling emboldened, you venture to speak again.

'Please forgive my intrusion; I seem to have lost my way.'

'Not at all,' she replies, 'you are most welcome here. I'm afraid I can offer you no refreshment, but please, do sit down.'

She indicates a small chair by the fireplace, and you take a seat, endeavouring to appear relaxed.

'I am sorry there is no fire,' says the young woman, 'but the aspect is so favourable that even without a fire, this room is habitable in many an early spring and late autumn morning to such a willing mind as mine. My plants, my books – of which I have been a collector from the first hour of my commanding a shilling – my writing-desk, and my works of charity and ingenuity, are all within my reach; or if indisposed for employment, if nothing but musing will do, I can scarcely see an object in this room which has not an interesting remembrance connected with it.'[10]

'Can this girl be sane?' you ask yourself.

'Everything is a friend,' she continues, with no regard for your evident lack of interest in what she has to say, 'or bears my thoughts to the outside world; and though there have been times of suffering; though my feelings have been often disregarded, and my comprehension undervalued; though I have known the pains of tyranny, of ridicule, and neglect, the *room* has been most dear to me, and I would not change its furniture for the handsomest in the house.'

You wonder who this mad girl in the attic can be.

'And this room will soon become dear to *you*,' she says, with a warm smile. 'In time, you will learn to love it as I do.'

'What do you mean?' you ask, a little alarmed by what she seems to be implying.

'You are to live with me now, Miss Bennet.'

'How do you know my name?' you demand, panic rising in your voice.

'Everyone knows your name, Miss Bennet; come now, no false modesty, please.'

You are about to protest, but are prevented.

'Oh yes, Miss Bennet,' she continues, 'I have read all about *you*! Miss Bennet this, Miss Bennet that! So interesting, so witty! Engaging, bold, spirited and handsome; such bright eyes, so lively; no fortune, no connections, no talents to speak of, but when did that ever stop Elizabeth Bennet?'

'What on earth do you mean?' you cry in alarm.

'You *know* what I mean!' she cries. 'Do you think it's easy for the rest of us? Forced to live in your shadow? Forever being compared, unfavourably, to *you*? Now that I've got you here, do you think I'm going to let you go? I might not be able to escape my prison, but at least the others will have a chance; Elinor Dashwood, Catherine Morland,[11] even your own poor sister Jane, even your own sister can never shine while she must walk beside you.'

'But that's ridiculous!' you cry. 'Everyone knows she's far more beautiful than…'

'Silence!' she cries before you can finish, and with that she composes herself, assumes an expression of purity and serenity, and goes back to her writing.

You are never allowed to leave and you eke out the rest of your days as your captor Fanny Price's prisoner, bored and neglected, until she smothers you to death one night with the oppressive weight of her nauseating meekness.

The End

You have failed. In the most insipid and banal way possible.

A failure to the end, you fail even in failing.

Tragic.

Correct.

Congratulations! You are quite right. You are, however, boring and smug.

 Deduct 100 FORTUNE POINTS for being dull.

Continue on page 118.

You make some slight observation on the dance; he replies, and is again silent. You are determined to make him speak however, and will not give up. After a pause of some minutes, you address him a second time with, 'It is your turn to say something now, Mr Darcy. I talked about the dance, and you ought to make some kind of remark on the size of the room, or the number of couples.'

He smiles.

'Do you talk by rule then, while you are dancing?' asks Mr Darcy.

He means to insult you but is unsuccessful. Instead you are amused by his attempt, and choose to retaliate not by denying, but conceding the point.

'Sometimes,' you reply with a smile. 'One must speak a little, you know. It would look odd to be entirely silent for half an hour together, and yet for the advantage of some, conversation ought to be so arranged as that they may have the trouble of saying as little as possible.'

From his change in expression, you see that the real meaning of your last comment is not lost upon him.

'Are you consulting your own feelings in the present case, or do you imagine that you are gratifying mine?' he replies.

'Both,' you reply archly, surprised at your own daring; 'for I have always seen a great similarity in the turn of our minds. We are each of an unsocial, taciturn disposition, unwilling to speak, unless we expect to say something that will amaze the whole room, and be handed down to posterity with all the éclat of a proverb.'

You are impressed with this latest display of your wit, even if nobody else is. Give yourself 10 CONFIDENCE POINTS and 10 INTELLIGENCE POINTS.

'This is no very striking resemblance of your own character, I am sure,' says he. 'How near it may be to mine, I cannot pretend to say.'

You had rather expected him to retaliate, and this gallant response leaves you at a momentary loss for words. You are silent till you have gone down the dance, when he asks you if you and your sisters do not very often walk to Meryton. You answer in the affirmative. You are pleased that he has provided you with the opportunity to broach the subject of Mr Wickham. You are extremely curious to hear what he has to say on the matter.

 Here is your chance to make a second attempt on Darcy's Shield of Pride. This time you select Impudence as your weapon. You've already failed once, so put a little effort into it.

Unable to resist the temptation, you add shortly afterwards, 'When you met us there the other day, we had just been forming a new acquaintance.'

The effect is immediate. A deeper shade of hauteur overspreads his features, but he says not a word.

 A passable first move.

Though blaming yourself for your own weakness, you cannot go on.

 Quitter.

89

At length Darcy speaks, and in a constrained manner says, 'Mr Wickham is blessed with such happy manners as may ensure his making friends – whether he may be equally capable of retaining them, is less certain.'

His sneering disdain disgusts you.

You decide to take another strike after all.

'He has been so unlucky as to lose your friendship,' you reply with emphasis, 'and in a manner which he is likely to suffer from all his life.'

Darcy makes no answer, and seems desirous of changing the subject.

Hardly a triumphant victory, is it? Step it up a bit.

At that moment Sir William Lucas appears and on perceiving Mr Darcy, stops with a bow of superior courtesy to compliment him on his dancing and his partner.

You sheathe your Impudence for the time being.

'I must hope to have this pleasure often repeated,' says Sir William, 'especially when a certain desirable event, my dear Miss Eliza,' he glances at your sister and Bingley, 'shall take place. What congratulations will then flow in! I appeal to Mr Darcy – but let me not interrupt you, sir.'

Sir William's allusion to his friend seems to strike Mr Darcy forcibly and his eyes are directed with a very serious expression towards Bingley and Jane. You feel keenly all the indiscretion of Sir William's so openly alluding to the general expectation of an imminent engagement being formed between Bingley and Jane, and grieve that Darcy should have been the one to hear it. You only hope, for Jane's sake, that whatever Darcy feels on the matter, Sir William's sentiments will not offend Bingley himself should he hear of them.

 Sir William Lucas is threatening Jane's marriage prospects, and by extension, your own. Deduct 10 FORTUNE POINTS and add 'Sir William Lucas' to your list of INFERIOR CONNECTIONS.

When you have recovered from Sir William's interruption, you turn once again to Darcy.

 You feel compelled to resume your attack.

After some moments' silence you suddenly exclaim, 'I remember hearing you once say, Mr Darcy, that you hardly ever forgave, that your resentment once created is unappeasable. You are very cautious, I suppose, as to its being created.'

'I am,' says he, with a firm voice.

'And never allow yourself to be blinded by prejudice?'

'I hope not.'

 You're not very good at this, are you?

He is giving very little away.

'It is particularly incumbent on those who never change their opinion,' you venture, growing ever bolder, 'to be secure of judging properly at first.'

'May I ask to what these questions tend?'

'Merely to the illustration of your character, I am trying to make it out,' you say, endeavouring to shake off your gravity and concerned lest you have gone too far.

 Coward.

'And what is your success?' replies Mr Darcy.

You shake your head. 'I do not get on at all. I hear such different accounts of you as puzzle me exceedingly.'

'I can readily believe,' he answers gravely, 'that reports may vary greatly with respect to me; and I could wish, Miss Bennet, that you are not to sketch my character at the present moment, as there is reason to fear that the performance would reflect no credit on either.'

You catch his meaning – he is referring, of course, to Mr Wickham – but you are unwilling to give up.

'But if I do not take your likeness now, I may never have another opportunity.'

 Is that the best you can do?

'I would by no means suspend any pleasure of yours,' he coldly replies.

 Deduct 10 INTELLIGENCE POINTS for failing, for the second time, to penetrate Darcy's Shield of Pride.

You say no more, and when the dance is over you part in silence, dissatisfied and angry at Darcy's obstinate silence on the subject of Wickham. To you, it merely betrays his guilt in the matter.

You then seek Jane who meets you with a smile of such sweet complacency, a glow of such happy expression, as sufficiently marks how well she is satisfied with the evening's developments. You listen with delight to the happy, though modest, hopes which she entertains of Bingley's regard, and say all in your power to heighten her confidence in it. Mr Collins then approaches you and tells you with great exultation that he has just made the discovery that Mr Darcy is related to Lady Catherine, and is on his way to pay his respects to him. You are horrified. You assure him that Mr Darcy would consider his addressing him without introduction as an impertinent freedom, rather than a compliment to his aunt. He listens to you with the determined air of following his own inclination, and with a low bow leaves you to attack Mr Darcy. Mr Darcy eyes him with unrestrained wonder, and when at last Mr Collins allows him time to speak, replies with an air of distant civility. Mr Collins, however, is not discouraged from speaking again. Mr Darcy's contempt seems abundantly increasing with the length of his second speech, and at the end of it he only makes him a slight bow, and moves another way.

Add 'Mr Collins' to your list of INFERIOR CONNECTIONS.

You turn your attention almost entirely on your sister and Mr Bingley, and what you see of them together makes you almost as happy as Jane. Your mother's thoughts are apparently bent the same way, for when you sit down to supper shortly afterwards, you are deeply vexed to find that your mother is talking to Lady Lucas freely, openly, and of nothing else but of her expectation that Jane should be soon married to Mr Bingley. In vain do you endeavour to check the rapidity of your mother's words for you perceive that the chief of it was overheard by Mr Darcy. You cannot help frequently glancing your eye at him and you see that he hears it all. The expression of his face changes gradually from indignant contempt to a composed and steady gravity. You blush and blush again with shame and vexation.

 Add 'Mother' to your list of INFERIOR CONNECTIONS.

When supper is over, singing is talked of, and you have the mortification of seeing your plain younger sister Mary, after very little entreaty, preparing to oblige the company with a song. Mary's powers are by no means fitted for such a display; her voice is weak, and her manner affected. You are in agonies. You look at Bingley's sisters, and see them making signs of derision at each other, and at Darcy, who continues to look impenetrably grave.

 Add 'Mary' to your list of INFERIOR CONNECTIONS.

You catch your father's eye in an attempt to entreat his interference, lest Mary should be singing all night. He takes the hint, and when Mary has finished her second song, says aloud, 'That will do extremely well, child. You have delighted us long enough. Let the other young ladies have time to exhibit.'

Mary, though pretending not to hear, is somewhat disconcerted, and you are very sorry for your father's insensitive speech.

 If there's any room left, add 'Father' to your ever-growing list of INFERIOR CONNECTIONS.

To you it appears that had your family made an agreement to expose themselves as much as they could during the evening, it would have been impossible for them to play their parts with more spirit, or finer success.

At length you arise to take leave, your mother invites the whole family to Longbourn and Bingley readily engages to wait on her after his return from London, whither, you learn, he is obliged to go tomorrow for a short time. You return home, and take to your bed, very glad indeed that the evening and its miseries are over at last.

———⊱◈⊰———

The next day opens a new scene at Longbourn: Mr Collins makes his declaration in form. It seems your miseries are not yet over after all. After securing a private audience with you, he begins.

'Almost as soon as I entered the house,' says he, 'I singled you out as the companion of my future life. But before I am run away with by my feelings on this subject, perhaps it will be advisable for me to state my reasons for marrying.'

The idea of Mr Collins, with all his solemn composure, being run away with by his feelings, makes you so near laughing that you cannot use the short pause he allows in any attempt to stop him from speaking further.

 Your sense of humour has never been more ill-timed. Add 'Ill-Timed Sense of Humour' to your FAILINGS.

His reasons for marrying are pragmatic – 'it is a right thing for every clergyman in easy circumstances to set the example of matrimony in his parish' – and since he is to inherit your father's estate, he feels it is only right to ask you. In addition to these powerful incentives, his esteemed patroness has instructed him to do so, and it therefore only remains (so he tells you with a flourish) for him to assure you in the most animated of language of 'the violence of his affection'.

It is absolutely necessary to interrupt him now.

To save your sisters and mother from being turned out of Longbourn after the unhappy but inevitable event of your father's death, turn to page 73 to accept Mr Collins. Your situation is critical.

To reject his offer, confident in your conviction that anything is to be preferred or endured rather than marrying without affection, turn to page 102.[12]

Incorrect.

Oh dear. You really are a disgrace to your sex.

 You are, however, charmingly irreverent. Collect 200 FORTUNE POINTS for refusing to conform to society's expectations of you, and add 'Charmingly Irreverent' to your list of ACCOMPLISHMENTS.

Continue on page 118.

Your curiosity is unexpectedly relieved when Mr Wickham begins the subject himself. After making sure that neither you nor anyone else in the neighbourhood feels any sentiment towards Mr Darcy beyond a general disgust at his pride, Wickham begins his account.

Wickham's reason for avoiding Darcy arises from a sense of very great ill-usage. To your astonishment you learn that, born in the same parish and within the same park, they passed the greatest part of their youth together. *Wickham's* father gave up everything to be of use to the late Mr Darcy, and devoted all his time to the care of the Darcy family property, Pemberley. He was highly esteemed by Mr Darcy as a most intimate, confidential friend and immediately before Wickham's father died, the late Mr Darcy gave him a voluntary promise of providing for young Wickham. He bequeathed him the best church living it was in his power to bestow; but you are horrified to learn that when the living next became available it was given elsewhere. You are appalled by what you hear, and your opinion of Darcy sinks lower and lower. According to Wickham, there was an informality in the terms of the bequest, and young Mr Darcy asserted that Wickham had forfeited all claim to it by extravagance and imprudence, though Wickham can accuse himself of having done nothing to deserve to lose it. You do not doubt him, and can hardly imagine it possible that one as affable and reasonable as Wickham could be accused of extravagance and imprudence.

Add 'Blind Partiality' to your list of FAILINGS.

It is much easier to believe that Mr Darcy could have manipulated the informality of the bequest to suit his own ends.

Add 'Wilful Prejudice' to your list of FAILINGS.

Wickham believes that Darcy was jealous of the attention paid to Wickham by his father after the death of Wickham's own. You are shocked and disgusted, but you suddenly remember Darcy's boasting at Netherfield of the implacability of his resentments, of his having an unforgiving temper. Mr Wickham's account confirms all that you have long suspected concerning Darcy. From almost the first moment you saw him you knew him to be a proud, disagreeable man, and nothing that he has done since has had any effect beyond confirming this first impression. You wonder that Wickham can bear to remain in the same county as Mr Darcy.

'I hope,' you venture, 'your plans in favour of Hertfordshire will not be affected by his being in the neighbourhood.'

'Oh! No – it is not for *me* to be driven away by Mr Darcy. If *he* wishes to avoid seeing *me*, he must go.'

You are very pleased to hear it. You are again deep in thought, struggling to take in the full meaning of what you have heard, and after a time you exclaim, 'To treat in such a manner, the godson, the friend, the favourite of his father! I wonder that the very pride of this Mr Darcy has not made him just to you!'

'It *is* wonderful,' replies Wickham, 'for almost all his actions may be traced to pride; and pride has often been his best friend.'

You are extremely surprised to hear Wickham defend the very man who has been the means of ruining his every prospect and rather wonder that Mr Wickham should *commend* his excessive and offensive pride.

'Can such abominable pride as his, have ever done him good?' you ask, doubtingly.

You have raised an important point.
Can such abominable pride ever do a man good?

If you think no, absolutely not, turn to page 111.

If you think yes, Darcy's pride does him credit,
turn to page 124.

To his great surprise and disappointment, you refuse him. You tear yourself away from his as quickly as you can lest you should change your mind and give in to your heart's desire and make an extremely imprudent match.

 Collect 100 FORTUNE POINTS for acting prudently. This might help you next time you fall for a woefully impoverished young man. But probably not.

Continue on page 125.

'You are too hasty, sir,' you cry. 'You forget that I have made no answer. Let me do it without further loss of time. Accept my thanks for the compliment you are paying me, but it is impossible for me to do otherwise than decline.'

You feel an immediate sense of relief at having made your refusal, and having made it clearly. You go to leave the room, but to your great surprise, Mr Collins stops you by assuring you, with a formal wave of the hand, that he knows it is usual with young ladies to reject, at first, the addresses of the man whom they secretly mean to accept, and that he is therefore by no means discouraged by what you have just said, and hopes to lead you to the altar before long. You are astonished and vexed by his response. In vain do you endeavour to make him see that you would not dare to risk your happiness on the chance of being asked a second time; it seems that nothing you can say can induce him to take your refusal seriously. He seems unable to accept the idea that you could reject what he considers to be such an attractive offer.

'It does not appear to me that my hand is unworthy of your acceptance,' says he. 'You should take it into further consideration that in spite of your manifold attractions, it is by no means certain that another offer of marriage may ever be made you. Your portion is unhappily so small that it will in all likelihood undo the effects of your loveliness and amiable qualifications.'

 Add 'Unhappily Small Portion' to your list of FAILINGS.

Your indignation at such an affront momentarily robs you of words and you are therefore unable to interrupt him before he has finished saying that he has concluded that you are not serious in your rejection of him, and that he attributes it to your wish of increasing his love by suspense, 'according to the usual practice of elegant females'.

To such perseverance in wilful self-deception, you can make no reply. You immediately withdraw in silence before you do or say something you will regret. You are resolved to apply to your father, whose negative might be uttered in such a decisive manner as to be definitive, and whose behaviour at least cannot be mistaken for the affectation and coquetry of an elegant female.

When Mrs Bennet discovers that you have refused Mr Collins, she goes directly to your father and you are summoned to the library.

'Come here, child,' cries your father as you appear. 'I have sent for you on an affair of importance. I understand that Mr Collins has made you an offer of marriage which you have refused. Is it true?'

You reply that it is.

'Very well. We now come to the point. Your mother insists upon your accepting it. Is not it so, Mrs Bennet?'

'Yes, or I will never see her again.'

'An unhappy alternative is before you, Elizabeth. From this day you must be a stranger to one of your parents. Your mother will never see you again if you do *not* marry Mr Collins, and I will never see you again if you *do*.'

Your father has redeemed himself and saved you from certain misery. Strike 'Father' from your list of INFERIOR CONNECTIONS and add him to your list of SUPERIOR CONNECTIONS. At last, some good fortune.

Your mother does not give up her point but coaxes and threatens you by turns; Mr Collins is in a state of angry pride and barely speaks to you at all. A respite is afforded when Charlotte Lucas comes to spend the day with the family, and her civility in listening to Mr Collins is a seasonable relief to you all.

The following morning a letter is delivered to Jane from Netherfield. You see your sister's countenance change as she reads it and a glance from Jane invites you to follow her upstairs. The letter is from Caroline Bingley and the news is not what you had hoped: the whole party has left Netherfield, and are on their way to town – none of them to return to Hertfordshire this winter.

Oh dear. Deduct 50 FORTUNE POINTS.

Caroline praises Darcy's sister Georgiana and expresses her hope that they will soon be sisters. Mr Bingley, she claims, admires Miss Darcy greatly already; and now that they are both in London, she believes it is just a matter of time before they are married. You, however, are not convinced, and treat the idea of Bingley never returning with the utmost contempt. You think that Miss Bingley sees that her brother is in love with Jane, *wants* him to marry Miss Darcy, and is doing her best therefore to separate Jane and Bingley. You cannot for a moment, however, suppose that those wishes, however openly or artfully spoken, could influence a young man as independent as Mr Bingley. You represent your feelings on the subject to Jane as forcibly as possible, and soon have the pleasure of seeing her hope restored.

During the chief of the following day, Charlotte is so kind as to listen to Mr Collins again but her kindness extends further than you have any conception of. It would seem that the object of Charlotte's kindness was nothing else than to secure you from any return of Mr Collins's addresses, by engaging them towards herself. The following morning Charlotte calls after breakfast to inform you that Mr Collins has proposed to her and that she has accepted him. Your astonishment is so great as to overcome at first the bounds of decorum, and you cannot help crying out, 'Engaged to Mr Collins! My dear Charlotte, impossible!'

You rather hope, than believe it to be impossible.

'Why should you be surprised, my dear Eliza? Do you think it incredible that Mr Collins should be able to procure any woman's good opinion, because he was not so happy as to succeed with you?'

Ouch. And this from one of your friends? Just imagine what your enemies think of you. Add 'No Real Friends' to your list of FAILINGS.

To think of Charlotte throwing away her happiness (as you see it) on such a man as Mr Collins distresses you deeply though you do your best to conceal the strength of your true feelings. Charlotte admits that Mr Collins is neither sensible nor agreeable; his society is irksome, and his attachment to her must be imaginary; but still he will be her husband. Without thinking highly either of men or of matrimony, she tells you, marriage has always been her object. You listen in silence, and are quite taken aback by her views. She argues that marriage is the only honourable provision for well-educated young women of small fortune, and however uncertain of giving happiness, must be their pleasantest preservative from want. This preservative she has now obtained; and at the age of twenty-seven, without having ever been handsome, she feels all the good luck of having ensured her future security. You can scarcely believe you are hearing your dearest childhood friend talking in this cold and calculated way, with no regard whatsoever for love. You feel as if you never knew her and are quite shaken.

'I am not romantic, you know,' she continues, 'I never was. I ask only a comfortable home; and considering Mr Collins's character, connections, and situation in life, I am convinced that my chance of happiness with him is as fair as most people can boast on entering the marriage state.'

'Undoubtedly,' you answer quietly; and after an awkward pause you return to the rest of the family.

Charlotte's representation of marriage depresses you. Consign her to your list of INFERIOR CONNECTIONS. She has sorely disappointed you.

Your disappointment in Charlotte makes you turn with fonder regard to your sister, for whose happiness you grow daily more anxious as Bingley has now been gone a week and nothing has been heard of his return.

A letter from Miss Bingley eventually arrives, and puts an end to doubt. The very first sentence conveys the assurance of their being all settled in London for the winter and the rest praises Miss Darcy's manifold attractions once more. You are very disappointed to hear that Bingley will return no more and while Jane accounts for it by believing that Bingley was never truly attached to her, *you* remain convinced his sisters and 'friend' have influenced him against her. You are very sorry for your sister and this latest circumstance only fuels yet further your angry feelings towards Mr Darcy and Bingley's sisters.

Mr Wickham's society is of material service in dispelling the gloom which the late perverse occurrences of Bingley's departure and Mr Collins's marriage plans have thrown on many of your family. You see Wickham often, and to his other recommendations is now added that of general unreserve. All that he has suffered from Mr Darcy is now openly acknowledged and publicly canvassed. Everybody is pleased to think how much they had always disliked Mr Darcy even before they had known anything of the matter. Wickham is a favourite throughout the neighbourhood, which only adds further charm to his attentions towards you.

Collect 10 CONFIDENCE POINTS.

On the following Monday, your mother has the pleasure of receiving her brother and his wife at Longbourn. Mr Gardiner is a sensible, gentlemanlike man, greatly superior to his sister, as much by nature as education. Mrs Gardiner is several years younger than Mrs Bennet and their other sister, Mrs Philips, and is an amiable, intelligent, elegant woman – a great favourite with all her Longbourn nieces.

During their stay, Wickham is often of your party and as Mrs Gardiner spent a considerable time, about ten years ago, in that very part of Derbyshire to which he belongs, they find they know many people in common and he is able to give her fresher intelligence of her former friends than she has been in the way of procuring. Since you value her opinion highly, it delights you to see your aunt enjoying Wickham's company. When you later acquaint her with Mr Darcy's treatment of Wickham, she tries to remember something of that gentleman's reputed disposition while a lad which might agree with your report, and is confident at last that she recollects having heard Mr Fitzwilliam Darcy formerly spoken of as a very proud, ill-natured boy.

 Wilful Prejudice and Blind Partiality clearly run in the family. Your own Blind Partiality towards your aunt, however, happily prevents you from noticing this. Hooray! Collect 10 CONFIDENCE POINTS *for having your own specious opinion speciously confirmed.*

Before leaving Hertfordshire, Mrs Gardiner cautions you against Mr Wickham. She reminds you of the imprudence of encouraging an attachment where there is an immediate want of fortune. You know that her advice is sound, though you do not readily wish to admit it: it irks you that want of fortune should be the sole means of preventing a match where there is a genuine meeting of minds. Though you tease her a little, however, you at last agree to do as she thinks wisest, or at least not *remind* your mother to invite him to the house so often.

 You're not getting any points for that feeble effort.

Your aunt is satisfied and now turns her thoughts and concern towards Jane.

'Do you think she would be prevailed on to go back with us?' she asks. 'A change of scene might be of service – and perhaps a little relief from home may be as useful as anything.'

Your mother's other sister, your aunt Philips, is apparently of the same view; at about this time Jane receives an invitation, extended to include you, to join her and your uncle on a trip to Bath.

Jane must now chose between London and Bath and asks your advice. You are not sure if it is wise for her to go to London where she might see Mr Bingley and be reminded of her recent disappointment.

If you think she should go to London anyway, confident that Mr Darcy would never suffer his friend to visit Jane in such a part of London as Gracechurch Street, turn to page 122.

If you think a change of scene would do her good, but that she might suffer from being separated from her closest family for so long, turn to page 112 to accompany her to London yourself.

If you think it best to stay away from London and the Bingleys and that the waters at Bath might restore Jane's spirits, turn to page 126 to accept the Philipses' invitation.

BELOW 150

Bad luck!

You could have been truly happy with Tom Lefroy but you are far too poor for him. Tom has five older sisters to support and is already indebted to his great-uncle for putting him through college and funding his studies in Law. The expectations of the whole family are laid on him.[13] He cannot possibly risk his future by attaching himself to someone as woefully poor as you.

This marriage was not to be. Heartbroken though you are, you must forget Tom Lefroy as best you can.

Continue on page 125.

You are not yet ready to learn the true value of pride and your opinion reflects your psychological naivety.

 Deduct 100 INTELLIGENCE POINTS.

So far his pride has only manifested itself in an air of conceited arrogance, however, so it's hardly surprising.

 Continue on your journey to gain the necessary experience to truly understand the concept of pride.

Continue with Mr Wickham's account on page 79.

You agree that a change of scene would be of great service to Jane but fear she would suffer from being separated from you at this difficult time. You think it best to accompany her to your aunt Gardiner's in London. It is decided: on Saturday morning you are to set forth.

You arrive at the Gardiners' house in Gracechurch Street in excellent time and soon feel that the change of scene is as welcome to you as it must be to Jane. Your first day in London passes pleasantly away, the morning in bustle and shopping, and the evening at one of the theatres. You are delighted with London and your spirits are greatly revived. You congratulate yourself, in the light of your aunt's advice, on not thinking of Wickham at all.

And in doing so immediately think of him. Walked right into that one, didn't you? Deduct 20 INTELLIGENCE POINTS.

The following evening you accompany your aunt and uncle to a large assembly in a fashionable part of town and you and Jane dress with care and attention, excited at the prospect of making new acquaintances. Shortly after your arrival, your host Mr King approaches and introduces you to a very gentlemanlike young Irishman from Dublin by the name of Mr Lefroy.[14] He seems to be about two or three and twenty, is tall, fair-haired, has a handsome and pleasing countenance, and a very intelligent and lively eye. You think he is perhaps the best-looking gentleman you have ever seen, even more handsome than Mr Wickham.

There you go again. Deduct a further 20 INTELLIGENCE POINTS.

Mr Lefroy has already completed a degree in Dublin and is about to study for the Bar in London; his address is good, and you feel yourself in high luck. You begin to feel that accompanying Jane to London was a very fine scheme indeed.

Collect 20 CONFIDENCE POINTS.

There is little leisure for speaking while you dance; but when you are seated at tea, you find Mr Lefroy as agreeable as you already gave him credit for being. He talks with fluency and spirit – and there is an archness and pleasantry in his manner which immediately piques your interest. You wish to know more of Mr Lefroy. After talking for some time he suddenly, and with mock-seriousness, apologizes for not having paid you the proper attentions expected of a partner.

'I have not yet asked you how long you have been in London; whether you were ever here before; whether you have been at the theatre, and the concert; and how you like the place altogether. I have been very negligent – but are you now at leisure to satisfy me in these particulars? If you are, I will begin directly.'

His tone and comic expression amuses you greatly and you are delighted to find that he considers the finer points of social etiquette as ridiculous as you do.

Collect 10 FORTUNE POINTS.

'You need not give yourself that trouble, sir,' you assure him with a smile, feeling that you understand one another well.

'No trouble, I assure you, madam,' says he, in reply. Then, forming his features into a set smile, and affectedly softening his voice, he adds, with a simpering air, 'Have you been long in London, madam?'

He is incorrigibly mischievous, but you like him all the more for it.

'Just two days, sir,' you reply, trying not to laugh at his perfect impression of a mannered gentleman of fashion.

Mr Lefroy affects astonishment. You take care to look about you and see that nobody who might be offended by his impression might be standing by, but though you see many a specimen who could have been the model for this representation, none is standing near enough to hear. You turn back to Mr Lefroy with a smile. You wonder what he would have to say about the sombre Mr Darcy, and when you imagine Mr Lefroy doing an impression of *him* it is all you can do to stop yourself from laughing out loud. He continues to ask you in his affected tone whether you have been to the theatre and to the concert, and how well you like London so far.

'I like it very well,' is the only reply you can manage; you are trying extremely hard to contain your laughter.

'Now I must give one smirk,' says he, 'and then we may be rational again.'

You turn away to laugh. His satire on London society could not have been more in keeping with your own thinking, and his manner of expression diverts you exceedingly.

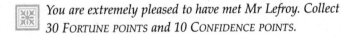

You are extremely pleased to have met Mr Lefroy. Collect 30 FORTUNE POINTS and 10 CONFIDENCE POINTS.

'I see what you think of me,' says he gravely, observing your

114

laughter. 'I shall make but a poor figure in your journal tomorrow.'

'My journal!' you exclaim in amusement, more and more diverted by Mr Lefroy. It has been many years since you kept a journal.

'Yes, I know exactly what you will say: "Last night, went to an assembly with my aunt; wore my sprigged muslin robe with blue trimmings – plain black shoes – appeared to much advantage; but was strangely harassed by a queer, half-witted man, who would make me dance with him, and distressed me by his nonsense."'

Mr Lefroy is apparently an expert in muslins. Can you claim the same? Take the following test for the chance to improve your FORTUNE SCORE.

What exactly is 'sprigged' muslin?

If you think it's a lightweight cotton cloth in a plain weave decorated with a design of sprigs of leaves or flowers, turn to page 87.

If you'd rather stick 'sprigs' in your eyes than have anything to do with sewing or fashion, turn to page 97.

Collect 50 INTELLIGENCE POINTS for so strictly observing discretion despite your burning curiosity.

You needn't have worried, however; the imprudent and indiscreet Mr Wickham is about to tell you himself anyway. The great impropriety of this happily escapes you at present.

Continue on page 98.

---

150 OR ABOVE

Congratulations!

Your FORTUNE SCORE is high enough to satisfy Mr Lefroy's high demands.

Unfortunately for you, by the time you have assessed your fortune, Mr Lefroy has been married off by his uncle to a wealthy Irish heiress from Wexford.[15]

You really are incredibly unfortunate (in all senses of the word). What did you do to deserve this?

Continue your mission on page 125, and consider going to church once in a while. You could use a little help.

Your conversation with Mr Lefroy continues. You assure him that you will *not* write in your journal that you were 'strangely harassed by a queer, half-witted man'. He gives you some hints as to what you *should* say, to which you reply archly that perhaps you keep no journal.

'Not keep a journal! How are your absent cousins to understand the tenor of your life in London without one? How are the civilities and compliments of every day to be related as they ought to be, unless noted down every evening in a journal? How are your various dresses to be remembered, and the particular state of your complexion, and curl of your hair, to be described in all their diversities, without having constant recourse to a journal?'

You laugh out loud this time, and are just on the point of replying when you are interrupted at this moment by Mrs Gardiner, with whom Mr Lefroy proceeds to converse with ease and elegance. Your admiration grows with every word he speaks, but you fear your aunt will not approve of this attachment: Mr Lefroy still has further studies to complete and has many financial obligations to his family.

Deduct 50 FORTUNE POINTS.

His prospects are therefore even worse than Wickham's.

Add 'Unfortunate Penchant for Penniless Gentlemen' to your list of FAILINGS.

You dance again; and you ask him what he thinks of books.

'I enjoy novels a great deal,' says he. 'But there has not been a tolerably decent one come out since *Tom Jones*.'[16]

You can hardly believe it. A shared admiration of your favourite novel, added to his handsome countenance, gentlemanly manner, wit, playfulness, and skill at dancing makes Thomas Langlois Lefroy the most charming man you have ever had the good fortune to meet, and when the assembly closes you part, on your side at least, with a strong inclination for continuing the acquaintance. Though you met but a few hours ago, you feel as if you have known him many months and go away with your head and heart full of Mr Lefroy.

You feel most fortunate to have met Mr Lefroy, and thank your lucky stars that at least one branch of your family has some tolerable connections. Add your host 'Mr King' to your list of Superior Connections. *You might not know him yourself but, quite frankly, you need all the help you can get.*

That evening you share your feelings for Mr Lefroy with Jane. 'I mean to confine myself in future to Mr Tom Lefroy, for whom I do not care sixpence,'[17] you say with good humour.

Jane is pleased that you are happy, and finds much to praise in him.

Jane's approbation further increases your Confidence *in Mr Lefroy. Award yourself 10* Confidence points.

Jane's approbation is totally indiscriminate. Deduct 10 Intelligence points *for valuing it.*

The following week you accompany your aunt to another ball, this time without Jane, who is prevented from attending by a violent toothache. You see Mr Lefroy again and feel that you have not been thinking of him with even the smallest degree of unreasonable admiration. He is everything you remembered him as being, and more. You are troubled to learn that he is to leave London the following Friday, but remind yourself that in affairs of the heart, much can happen in a few short days.

You return home that evening, flushed with happiness and wine, and Jane asks you how the evening passed.

'I am almost afraid to tell you how my Irish friend and I behaved,' you tease her. 'Imagine to yourself everything most profligate and shocking in the way of dancing and sitting down together. I *can* expose myself however, only *once more*,' you reassure her, 'because he leaves the country soon after next Friday.'[18]

'Take care, Lizzy,' cautions Jane. 'However attached to you he may be himself, with studies to complete, and obligations to his family, he is not necessarily free to pay his attentions where he wishes.'

You know she is right, though you do not wish to admit it. Her advice reminds you of that given to you by your aunt Gardiner as she cautioned you against Mr Wickham and though you are familiar with the ways of the world and what they must mean for you, this does not prevent you from being vexed by them.

Your happiness is once again threatened by your acute lack of Fortune. Realizing this causes you to lose a further 10 Fortune points. You curse your unlucky stars. They do not appreciate being cursed. You lose a further 10 Fortune points. Whoops.

Though you promise to, you cannot hide your admiration for Mr Lefroy; his manifold attractions are more persuasive than Jane's reasoning. He can hide his affections no better than you, and before his departure from London he pays you a visit and makes you an offer of marriage.

If you wish to accept his attractive offer, you must consult your Fortune score to see if you are eligible.

If your score is 150 or above, turn to page 117.

If it is below 150, turn to page 110.

If you wish to refuse him, conscious of his lack of Fortune and the further stress that more years of study will lay upon it, turn to page 101 and steel your heart against him.

You approve of your aunt Gardiner's scheme and tell her you are confident Jane will accept the invitation.

Although you are certain in your belief that Mr Darcy would never allow Bingley to call on Jane in such a part of London as Gracechurch Street, you still do not consider the situation entirely hopeless. It is possible, and sometimes you think it probable, that Bingley's affection might be reanimated, and the influence of his friends successfully combated by the more natural influence of Jane's attractions, should they meet again.

Jane accepts your aunt's invitation with pleasure; and they set off for London in high spirits the following Saturday. As she leaves, you urge Jane to write as soon as possible, secretly hoping that she will soon be able to send favourable news of Bingley. You will miss your sister, and once you have watched the carriage leave, you turn back to the house with a heavy heart. With Jane gone and Charlotte soon to follow, you will soon be at a loss for intelligent company. You therefore resolve to apply yourself to your work with more than usual vigour so as to leave no time for sad reflections.

Congratulations. You have completed Stage Two.

Your judgement remains contemptible, however, and your chances of marrying prudently therefore marginal at best.

Go to your room and don't come out till you're ready to consider the consequences of your actions like a real adult.

Then proceed to Stage Three on page 143.

Don't be stupid, his pride is extremely objectionable. If you can already appreciate the value of his pride what can you possibly hope to learn from your interaction with Mr Darcy? You are displaying an inappropriate level of psychological maturity.

 Stop trying to be clever, and deduct 20 INTELLIGENCE POINTS for your impertinence.

Continue with Mr Wickham's account on page 79.

You judge it best to remove yourself from London and all its reminders of your recent, but sadly demised, happiness. Jane is prevailed upon to stay by your aunt and uncle, and as you take leave of her, it gives you comfort to think that though you have not yet met with them, she must surely soon be reunited with the Bingleys. Reflecting on this gives you great pleasure and you journey home to Longbourn in good spirits.

When you are safely back in Hertfordshire your thoughts turn to Charlotte and her forthcoming marriage to your cousin Mr Collins. You will miss her friendship and society dearly, and feel a great deal of pity and compassion for her when you imagine what her life as Mrs Collins will be like. It was her choice, however; she has chosen her fate and there is nothing to do now but wait for the wedding to seal it.

Congratulations! You have now completed Stage Two.

Your acute lack of FORTUNE continues to jeopardize all hopes of future happiness however, so don't start celebrating just yet.

Then proceed to Stage Three on page 143.

You decide that it would be best for Jane not to go to London, but agree that a change of scene would do her good. You both accept the invitation from your aunt and uncle Philips and all set off for Bath the following Saturday.

You make your appearance in the Lower Rooms on the third evening of your visit; and here fortune is favourable to you. The master of ceremonies introduces to you a very gentlemanlike young man by the name of Henry Tilney.[19] He seems to be about four or five and twenty, is rather tall, has a pleasing countenance, a very intelligent and lively eye, and, if not quite handsome, is very near it.

Beggars can't be choosers, you know. You are only 'tolerable' yourself, remember? Lower your expectations a little or you'll never get a husband. Add 'Unreasonably High Expectations' to your list of FAILINGS.

He is a clergyman of a very respectable family in Gloucestershire whose mother, you learn, died some years ago. Though he is not as handsome as Mr Wickham, there is something in his manner that speaks of a quickness that Wickham was sometimes without and you feel all the good fortune of meeting him now, after your aunt's recent caution against Mr Wickham, when you are most in need of distraction and diversion.

Collect 10 bonus FORTUNE POINTS.

Mr Tilney introduces you and Jane to his father and sister and you are pleased with them both. Eleanor is every bit as

126

charming as her brother and has a good figure and pretty face. Their father, General Tilney, is a very handsome man, of a commanding aspect, past the bloom, but not past the vigour of life. You introduce them to the Philipses and everyone is delighted with each other.

'What a handsome family they are!' Jane whispers to you as the Tilneys are talking to your aunt and uncle. You couldn't agree more.

 Add 'The Tilneys' to your list of SUPERIOR CONNECTIONS.

You dance and converse with Mr Tilney for most of the evening, and are impressed and charmed by his wit and intelligence. You discover that he loves the gothic novels of Mrs Radcliffe, and he recommends one or two of them for you to read. It is a genre of literature you have thought laughable in the past, but a recommendation from Mr Tilney is enough to make you reconsider it. You go home that night thinking of Mr Tilney, and have high hopes of meeting him again at tomorrow evening's cotillion ball.

For once, your hopes are not disappointed.

 It's a miracle. Collect 10 bonus FORTUNE POINTS.

When you enter the ballroom the following evening you soon find yourself addressed and solicited to dance by Mr Tilney and you grant his request with pleasure.

From this time forward, you spend as many of your days as possible with the Tilneys, and your regard for the brother gradually increases. You obtain copies of Mrs Radcliffe's novels *The Romance of the Forest* and *The Mysteries of Udolpho* as recommended, and find that you cannot put them down. Against all your better judgement you are forced to confess yourself a fan of gothic literature. You remember Darcy's speech on the accomplishments of women and the necessity of expanding the mind through extensive reading and wonder what he would think of you if he could see you now. Somehow you doubt that his idea of 'extensive reading' includes the novels of Mrs Radcliffe. You care not, however; you have little respect for Mr Darcy's opinion, and hold Mr Tilney's in the highest esteem. Gothic literature is a guilty pleasure in which you find you are more than happy to indulge.

One morning, just as you are reflecting on how pleasant it is for you to now have friends in Bath, Miss Tilney informs you of her father's plans to leave town by the end of the week.

Deduct 10 FORTUNE POINTS for your extraordinary bad luck.

You are very sorry for it, but you do not have long to lament your bad luck, for Miss Tilney proceeds to invite you to accompany them to their family home, Northanger Abbey.

Fortune's wheel is turning fast. Collect 20 points.

Having recently read a great deal of gothic literature, you find the prospect of staying in a real-life abbey quite exciting. You are reluctant to leave Jane, but she assures you that she is well and happy, and greatly enjoying the society that Bath affords. Your aunt and uncle agree to part with you, and you therefore accept Eleanor's invitation and set off in Henry's curricle at the appointed time the following Saturday.[20]

You arrive at the abbey in good time and Miss Tilney shows you to your apartment. It is all disappointingly modern and not at all what you have been led to expect from the gothic novels you have read. Despite yourself, you cannot help feeling a little disappointed.

Who do you think you are? A character in a novel? Idiot. Deduct 50 INTELLIGENCE POINTS.

You dress quickly for dinner and hurry down to the drawing room where the general is pacing, his watch in his hand and, on the very instant of your entering, pulls the bell with violence and orders: 'Dinner to be on the table directly!' His temper seems unreasonably short and you begin to wonder whether your stay at Northanger is going to be quite as pleasant as you had anticipated. You had not thought it possible, but General Tilney seems to be even more bad-tempered than Mr Darcy.

The following morning Mr Tilney leaves you for London, where business will keep him for some days.

Just your luck. Deduct 10 FORTUNE POINTS.

You are a little disappointed to see him go, but you mood is brightened when Eleanor and the general propose a tour of the abbey. You begin with the gardens, and before long you come to a narrow path that winds through a thick grove of old Scotch firs. It is dark and shady and you are struck by its gloomy aspect. To your surprise, the general excuses himself from attending you, saying that he prefers to be in the sun, and will meet you by another course.

'I am particularly fond of this spot,' says Miss Tilney as you turn into the grove. 'It was my mother's favourite walk.'

Mrs Tilney is so rarely mentioned in the family that your interest is piqued by this tender remembrance. It seems to you as a little odd that the general should have excused himself from entering the grove if it was Mrs Tilney's favourite walk, but you think little of it. Miss Tilney goes on to tell you that she was only thirteen when her mother died, and you are struck by the sadness of the story. You are curious to know more about Mrs Tilney and with every answer your questions receive, your interest in her augments. From what Eleanor says, and from your own observations of the general's temper, you begin to feel persuaded that Mrs Tilney was unhappy in marriage. Your instincts tell you it must have been so.

> Your instincts are extremely unreliable. Deduct 20
> INTELLIGENCE POINTS for failing to realize it and add
> 'Extremely Unreliable Instincts' to your list of FAILINGS.

The end of the path brings you directly upon the general, and you find yourself again obliged to walk with him. Though you smile and talk with him as before, you cannot put your thoughts concerning Mrs Tilney's unhappiness entirely from your mind. You wish to know more about her and the circumstances of her death, and resolve to ask Eleanor for further details when next you are alone.

You finish your tour of the gardens and return to the abbey where your tour resumes. You are curious to see more of the surroundings in which Mr Tilney was raised, and to learn more about him. When you come across a portrait of Mr Tilney, you cannot help stopping to admire it for some moments. It is a striking resemblance, with such a smile over the face as you have sometimes seen when he looked at you. All at once, you feel a regard for Mr Tilney much stronger than that which you have felt before this moment and you begin to hope he will not be detained in London too long.

Your tour continues and you ascend the chief staircase and turn in an opposite direction from the gallery in which your room lies. Miss Tilney is just about to open a door to the left when her father the general comes forward and calls her hastily, and rather angrily back, demanding to know where she is going, and affirming that you have surely already seen all that can be worth your notice. He clearly wishes to conceal something, and what that something is, a short sentence of Miss Tilney's seems to point out: 'I was going to take you into what was my mother's room – the room in which she died'. You wonder what Mrs Radcliffe would have to say about the general's behaviour. He seems reluctant to venture any place that might remind him of his late wife, and you begin to wonder if it does not spring from his own sense of guilt concerning his behaviour towards her during her illness. Your suspicions are aroused and you grow more and more convinced that the general was a hard, unfeeling husband.

Add 'Distastefully Suspicious' to your list of FAILINGS.

You venture, when next alone with Miss Tilney, to express your wish of being permitted to see her mother's room, as well as all the rest of that side of the house; and she promises to attend you there, whenever there is a convenient hour. You guess at her meaning: that the general must be away from home before that room can be entered. Such hints only compound your growing suspicions. You ask her if the room remains as it was, and when she replies in the affirmative, you cannot refrain from going on to ask if she was with her mother to the last.

'No,' replies Miss Tilney, 'I was unfortunately from home. Her illness was sudden and short; and it was all over before I arrived.'

Your blood runs cold with the suggestions which naturally spring from these words. Could Henry's father …? Could it be possible? It hardly bears thinking about, but you find that you cannot put the awful possibility from your mind. You resolve at last to discover the truth, and think that your best chance of success lies in gaining admittance to Mrs Tilney's room, which might yet hold some clue as to what happened in those final days leading up to her death. To your disappointment, though you hope to be shown her apartment soon, no opportunity arises.

To make an attempt on the forbidden door alone, turn to page 137. To do so is to risk being caught by the general, however, and if he really is a murderer, who knows what he might do to you?

To play it safe and wait for Miss Tilney to accompany you, turn to page 83.

You are in such a shock that, without knowing what you do, you accept him. He walks away again immediately to join the other dancers as they prepare to begin, and you are left to fret over your own want of presence of mind.

You take your place in the set, and read in your neighbours' looks their amazement in beholding you standing opposite Mr Darcy. That the man who had not thought you handsome enough to dance with when you first met should now actively seek you out is surprising indeed and you know not how to account for it. Though you dislike Darcy, you cannot deny that it is a most unexpected honour to be asked to dance with him.

In spite of yourself, your vanity is gratified. Award yourself 10 bonus CONFIDENCE POINTS.

Vanity is still a sin. Deduct 20 FORTUNE POINTS.

You both dance for some time without speaking a word.

You begin to imagine that your silence is to last through the two dances.

133

If you decide to play him at his own game and resolve not to say a word, turn to page 78.

If you fancy that it would be the greater punishment to your partner to oblige him to talk, turn to page 88 and begin your attack.

———⟫◆⟪———

You decline as politely as you can and take a walk about the assembly. You stop to observe the dancing and it is some moments before you perceive that Mr Darcy has not been thwarted in his intention of partaking in the dance and is, in fact, dancing with none other than Charlotte Lucas. You are somewhat taken aback that the man who had not thought *you* handsome enough to tempt him to dance that first evening, has been tempted by one who everyone agrees is extremely plain.

This is a blow indeed; Charlotte really is undeniably ugly.
Deduct 20 CONFIDENCE POINTS.

When you have regained your composure you begin to pity your poor friend the misfortune of having to converse with one so proud and humourless as Mr Darcy, and your thoughts turn once more to Mr Wickham. You consider when you might reasonably hope to see him again, and it is with pleasant reflections upon this anticipated event that you pass the rest of the evening.

The following day your hopes are rewarded with an early visit from the very same Mr Wickham. You take a walk about the garden and he attempts to excuse himself for his absence the previous evening.

Before long, he makes a formal declaration of his love for you. Mr Wickham is so disliked by Darcy that he fears your marriage might harm Jane's chances with that man's friend, Mr Bingley. Your thoughtful Mr Wickham therefore entreats you to journey with him to Gretna Green so that you might seal your love at the earliest opportunity, with the least inconvenience to your family.

Such consideration for those closest to you only serves to increase your love for him, and you agree to elope that very evening.

 This is an uncharacteristically stupid thing to do. Deduct 50 INTELLIGENCE POINTS.

Continue on page 12.

You decide to attempt the forbidden door alone and at four o'clock you retire to dress half an hour earlier than usual. You find yourself alone in the gallery before the clocks cease to strike. You slip with the least possible noise through the folding doors of the gallery, and without stopping, hurry forward to the door in question. The lock yields to your hand. On tiptoe you enter, and the room is before you. You see a large, well-proportioned apartment, a handsome bed, mahogany wardrobes, and neatly painted chairs, on which the warm beams of a western sun gaily pour through two sash windows. You are shocked at first, and then deeply mortified. You hardly know what scene of horror you expected to behold, or what possible proof of the general's cruelty could ever have been found there; but it is clear that you have been grossly mistaken in everything. Common sense returns to you and you feel bitterly ashamed of yourself. You feel that none of this ever would have happened if you hadn't been influenced by Mrs Radcliffe's novels, and you regret the day you ever set eyes on them.

Add 'Deplorable Weakness for Gothic Literature' to your list of FAILINGS and deduct 50 INTELLIGENCE POINTS.

You are sick of exploring, and want only to be safe in the solitude of your own room. You are on the point of retreating, when the sound of footsteps stops you in your tracks. To be found there, even by a servant, would be unpleasant; but by the general, much worse. You listen, but the sound has ceased. Resolving not to lose a moment, you pass through the door and close it behind you. At that instant a door underneath is hastily

opened and someone begins to ascend the stairs with swift steps.
You have no power to move. With a feeling of panic you fix your
eyes on the staircase and in a few moments are faced with Mr
Tilney.

 You really are EXTRAORDINARILY unlucky. Deduct 50
FORTUNE POINTS.

You are extremely astonished to see him, and know not how to
even begin explaining yourself to him.

'How came you here? How came you up that staircase?' you
ask hastily in some confusion.

 It's his house, he can go where he likes. Deduct 10
INTELLIGENCE POINTS for being so rude.

He looks astonished too, and explains in a tone of great
surprise that it is the nearest way from the stable yard to his own
chamber. You recollect yourself, blush, and can say no more.
You move on towards the gallery, eager to be gone, but Mr
Tilney stops you by asking in turn, how *you* came to be there.
Avoiding his eye, you explain that you have been to see his
mother's room and then do your best to change the subject.

 You're not getting out of it that easily. Deduct 10
INTELLIGENCE POINTS for trying.

Mr Tilney is taken in by your attempt to change the subject
and asks you what you thought of his mother's room. He asks
you if Eleanor sent you to see it and 'No' is your only reply. Your
sense of mortification grows with every passing moment.

Deduct 20 CONFIDENCE POINTS.

You say a silent prayer, asking for the earth to open and swallow you whole. Nothing happens.

 Deduct 20 INTELLIGENCE POINTS.

After a short silence, during which Mr Tilney closely observes you, he asks whether your curiosity to see the room proceeded from Eleanor's description of their mother's character, and whether Eleanor has talked of her a great deal.

'Yes. No. That is, not so much,' you reply, floundering. 'But what she did say was very interesting. Her dying so suddenly,' you continue with some hesitation, 'and none of you being at home…'

You can hardly believe you have just all but admitted your real reasons for being in this part of the abbey. Henry is quick to catch your meaning, and asks whether, from these circumstances, you have inferred the probability of some negligence, or, perhaps, something much worse. You are mortified beyond expression and can make no answer.

 Deduct 50 CONFIDENCE POINTS.

Mr Tilney explains that though the seizure which ended in his mother's death *was* sudden, the malady itself was one from which she had often suffered. During the progress of her disorder he saw her repeatedly, though Eleanor *was* absent, and at such a distance that sadly, when she retuned home, Mrs Tilney had died.

'But your father,' you ask, 'was *he* afflicted?'

You just can't let it go, can you?

'For a time, greatly so,' Mr Tilney replies. 'His value of her was sincere; and, if not permanently, he was truly afflicted by her death.'

'I am very glad of it,' you reply.

 Lord above, can you not hold your tongue? Deduct a further 20 INTELLIGENCE POINTS.

'If I understand you rightly,' replies Mr Tilney in some dismay, 'you had formed a surmise of such horror as I have hardly words to… Dear Miss Bennet, consider the dreadful nature of the suspicions you have entertained. What have you been judging from? Remember the country and the age in which we live. Remember that we are English, that we are Christians. Dearest Miss Bennet, what ideas have you been admitting?'

 You have deeply offended one of the few SUPERIOR CONNECTIONS you have. Deduct 30 INTELLIGENCE POINTS. What is wrong with you? Add 'Extremely Bad House Guest' to your list of FAILINGS.

You return to your room in shame and embarrassment. It is not only with yourself that you are sunk – but with Henry too. Your folly has been exposed to him, and he must despise you forever. You earnestly regret ever having read Mrs Radcliffe's novels, and cannot help but laugh at the bitter irony that it was Mr Tilney who introduced you to them in the first place. You vow never to pick one up again for as long as you live. You hope that in time, Henry will learn to forgive you, and your indiscretion will be forgotten.

<hr />

The following morning Eleanor comes to you in great distress to inform you that the general has recollected an engagement that takes the whole family away on Monday. Tomorrow morning is fixed for your leaving, and no servant will be offered you. It is clear that you have offended the general in some way and it seems to you only too likely that he has somehow learnt of your suspicions regarding his part in his wife's death. You are utterly mortified, and return home to Longbourn certain that you will never see Henry again.

 Your appalling and contemptible judgement has ruined what little chance you had of happiness with Mr Tilney. Deduct 50 INTELLIGENCE POINTS and 50 FORTUNE POINTS.

You long to see Jane, but when you left Bath to visit the Tilneys, she travelled on to stay with the Gardiners in London. You are sure she will send you news by letter soon, however, and every morning is spent watching out for the post.

The company and conversation of your father helps you to forget your recent disappointment and before long you learn not to think of Mr Tilney. You wouldn't want to live in an abbey anyway.

 Nice try, but nobody's fooled.

Your thoughts soon turn towards Charlotte and her forthcoming marriage to your cousin Mr Collins. You will miss her friendship and society dearly, and feel a great deal of pity and compassion for her when you imagine what her life as Mrs Collins will be like. It was her choice, however; she has chosen her fate and there is nothing to do now but wait for the wedding to seal it.

Congratulations! You have successfully completed Stage Two.

You will never get a husband if you carry on as you have done at Northanger Abbey. You're going to have to try a LOT harder.

Then proceed to Stage Three on page 145
and pull yourself together.

STAGE THREE

$\mathcal{T}$HE DAY OF Charlotte and Mr Collins's wedding approaches and on her final night of liberty Miss Lucas comes to say goodbye. She invites you to Hunsford and though you foresee little pleasure in the visit, you consent to be of the party when Sir William and Maria visit her in March. The wedding takes place and the bride and bridegroom set off for Kent from the church door. You are sorry to see your friend go.

The following day, you receive a letter from Jane in London. You had hoped to hear something of the Bingleys but your hopes are disappointed. A further four weeks pass before you receive news from Jane that Miss Bingley has finally visited her and that her manner towards your sister was greatly altered when she did. She implied to Jane that Mr Bingley knows she is in town, but is kept away by his partiality for Miss Darcy; and furthermore, that Bingley is never to return to Netherfield and will most likely give up the house. In the light of this, all hope for Mr Bingley and Jane is now absolutely over; and Mr Bingley's character sinks in your estimation on every review of it.

About this time Mrs Gardiner reminds you in a letter of your promise not to encourage Mr Wickham's attentions. She requires information about him and you have such to send as might rather give contentment to your aunt than to yourself. You have heard from your aunt Philips that Wickham has been paying his attentions to someone else. The sudden acquisition of ten thousand pounds is the most remarkable charm of the young lady, Miss King, to whom he is now rendering himself agreeable. His apparent partiality for you has subsided.

 Dear, oh dear. You can't even hold a man like Wickham's interest. Deduct 20 CONFIDENCE POINTS.

Though you cannot help feeling something very near jealousy when you hear the news, your sisters Kitty and Lydia take Wickham's defection much more to heart than you do. They are young in the ways of the world, and not yet open to the mortifying conviction that handsome young men must have something to live on as well as the plain.

 Collect 20 INTELLIGENCE POINTS for your awareness of the ways of the world and the dire disadvantage at which they put you.

March arrives and you set off to visit Charlotte at Hunsford with Sir William and Charlotte's sister, Maria. You spend the night at the Gardiners' house in London on your way and are pleased to see that Jane does not suffer from her disappointments: she is as healthful and lovely as ever. The day passes away most pleasantly and that evening you have the unexpected happiness of an invitation to accompany your uncle and aunt Gardiner in a tour of pleasure which they propose taking in the summer.

'We have not quite determined how far it shall carry us,' says your aunt, 'but, perhaps, to the Lakes.'

Your acceptance of the invitation is most ready and grateful. You feel all the advantage of having something to look forward to, and feel certain that the picturesque beauty of the area will distract you from all thoughts of Wickham.

'My dear, dear aunt,' you rapturously cry, 'what delight! What felicity! You give me fresh life and vigour. Adieu to disappointment and spleen. What are men to rocks and mountains?'

Good question. A trip to the Lakes is likely to prove a great test of your appreciation of the picturesque. Take the following **Picturesque Appreciation Test** to see if you are truly worthy of a trip to the Lake District.

Which of the following best describes you?

a) You are not really fond of nettles, thistles or heath blossoms. You prefer tall and flourishing trees to those which are crooked and blasted; neat to ruined cottages; and snug farmhouses to Gothic watchtowers.[21]

b) You are fond of nettles and thistles but not heath blossoms; and though you quite like Gothic watchtowers in principle, you wouldn't want to live in one.

c) You have read William Gilpin's essays on the picturesque forty times over and admire a good view so much that if it were interrupted by something that did not perfectly accord with your idea of the picturesque, you would immediately set about destroying it; even if that something were the entire city of Bath.[22]

If you answered a), turn to page 178.

If you answered b), turn to page 223.

If you answered c), turn to page 196.

You gratefully accept the colonel and do your best to ignore the objections of your conscience. Although you do not love him, his fortune will save you and your sisters from ruin when your father dies and you are turned out of your house by Mr Collins.

When Mr Darcy finds out the following day, he is so angry with his cousin that he challenges him to a duel. All is uproar at Rosings. Lady Catherine is distracted. She cannot believe that anyone could fight over such a woman as you, let alone *two* gentlemen from *her own* family. She drives over in her carriage and demands an audience with you. You meet her at the garden gate.

'You will *not* marry *either* of my nephews,' says she, without any introduction. 'Do I make myself clear Miss Bennet?'

'Certainly,' you reply. 'And if they should both hit their targets, I won't have to.'

'I will not tolerate this!' she roars, before departing in a cloud of dust.

You return indoors to find Charlotte attending to Mr Collins who appears to have fainted. You step over him and make your way upstairs.

You rise before dawn the following morning, and dress quickly. You don't want to miss the duel, and since the winner will in all probability be your future husband, you think it prudent to be the first to know *which* cousin it will be.

When you arrive at the appointed grassy clearing in the woods of Rosings Park, you see across the way from you (through a heavy morning mist) a small gathering of people. It seems that you are not to be the only spectator. Amongst those gathered are Lady Catherine, her daughter, and even Mr

Collins. He offers Lady Catherine his unwavering support in the face of these difficult circumstances by way of standing too close to her, hanging upon her arm, and crying a great deal.

You all wait in an agony of suspense, until at last the gentlemen arrive. They stand together in the middle of the clearing, back to back. Mr Collins faints again. The gentlemen begin their ten paces: one, two, three…

'And all of this for me!' you think, wondering if it is absolutely necessary for one of them to have to die for this dispute to be settled.

Four, five, six… they continue their paces.

You are not sure which cousin you would like to win. Mr Darcy is insufferable, it's true, but you can't deny that it was very gallant of him to challenge the colonel to a duel for your sake.

Seven, eight, nine…

They are only upon the ninth pace, when you are greatly surprised by the sound of a gunshot.

'Foul play!' is your first thought, and what with the general commotion that ensues, it is quite some moments before you realize that it is *you* who has been shot – and by none other than Lady Catherine. She really meant it when she said you wouldn't marry either of her nephews. At the sight of your own blood, you swoon to the ground.

'What have you done!' cries Darcy, as he runs to your aid. He sees that you are hit, and falls to his knees in an agony of grief.

Turning again to his aunt he shouts 'How could you!' and then, aiming his pistol at his aunt, he shoots her dead.

Not to be outdone, the colonel runs to you too.

'Get away from her!' cries Darcy. 'You didn't love her like I did!'

Mr Darcy shoots his cousin in a jealous rage and then, saving the last bullet for himself, puts the pistol in his mouth and pulls the trigger. He falls down dead upon you just before your own demise and you are united in death as you could never be in life. At least in heaven he needn't worry about the inferiority of your connections.

THE END

United though you are, this does not constitute a marriage, happy or otherwise.

You have failed.

The following day you leave London for Kent, satisfied that Jane is happy and healthy. At length you reach the village of Hunsford and the parsonage is discernible and Mr Collins and Charlotte appear at the door. With no other delay than Mr Collins's pointing out the neatness of the entrance, you are taken into the house.

You were prepared to see him in his full glory; and you cannot help fancying that in displaying the good proportions of the room, its aspect and its furniture, he addresses himself particularly to you as if wishing to make you feel what you have lost in refusing him. You certainly cannot deny that everything is more handsome than you had expected but you remain certain that not even the handsomest parsonage in the world could make you regret refusing Mr Collins. Your cousin then invites you to take a stroll in the garden from where you get a clear view of his patroness Lady Catherine's estate, Rosings Park. It is a handsome modern building, well situated on rising ground. You cannot help thinking of Lady Catherine's nephew Mr Darcy as you look on Rosings and all its grandness. You imagine that he must feel quite at home in such pompous and stately surroundings and dread to think what his own estate of Pemberley looks like.

'We dine at Rosings twice every week,' boasts Mr Collins, 'and are never allowed to walk home. Lady Catherine's carriage is regularly ordered for us. I *should* say, *one* of her ladyship's carriages, for she has several.'

Maria and Sir William seem impressed by Mr Collins's boast, but you cannot imagine what Lady Catherine could want with more than one carriage when there are just two in the family.

The following day Mr Collins's triumph is complete when Lady Catherine, as anticipated, sends an invitation to dinner. Scarcely anything else is talked of the whole day.

 It's going to be a LONG six weeks.

You wonder how Charlotte can bear to spend every day of her life in such a way.

When evening comes the weather is fine and you have a pleasant walk of about half a mile across the park to Rosings. As you ascend the steps to the hall, Maria's alarm at the prospect of meeting a woman as grand as Lady Catherine increases, and even Sir William does not look perfectly calm. *Your* courage, however, does not fail you.

 At least one of you has some sense. Collect 10 INTELLIGENCE POINTS.

You have heard nothing of Lady Catherine that tells of any extraordinary talents or miraculous virtue, and the mere stateliness of money and rank you think you can witness without trepidation. When Charlotte introduces you to Lady Catherine and her daughter Anne, you find yourself quite equal to the scene, and can observe the two ladies before you composedly. Lady Catherine is a tall, large woman, with strongly marked features, which might once have been handsome. Miss de Bourgh is pale and sickly; her features, though not plain, are insignificant; and she speaks very little.

 Clearly a member of the Darcy family.

Though the company leaves a lot to be desired, the dinner is exceedingly handsome. After dinner you return to the drawing room with the ladies of the group, where there is little to be done but listen to Lady Catherine talk. When she eventually runs out of things to say about herself, she asks you a few questions about your family. She is disgusted to discover that you never had a governess.

 Add 'No Governess' to your list of FAILINGS.

She is likewise shocked to learn that all five of your sisters are out in society at once.

 Add 'All Five Sisters Out at Once' to your list of FAILINGS.

Discovering that you can't draw is the last straw, and she abruptly ends the conversation. You play cards for the rest of the evening and though you find the conversation decidedly stupid you derive some pleasure at least from repeatedly beating Lady Catherine at whist. The carriage is at last offered, gratefully accepted, and you and your party return to the parsonage.

Sir William stays only a week at Hunsford; but his visit is long enough to convince him of his older daughter's being most comfortably settled, and of her possessing such a husband and such a neighbour as are not often met with.

 That's for sure.

Despite the evenings spent at Rosings, upon the whole you spend your time comfortably enough at Hunsford, in conversation with Charlotte, or walking alone.

In this quiet way the first fortnight of your visit soon passes away. Then you learn that Mr Darcy is expected at Rosings for Easter and can hardly believe your bad luck.

You curse your unlucky stars.

They do not appreciate being cursed.

You lose 10 FORTUNE POINTS. That'll teach you.

Darcy brings with him his cousin, a Colonel Fitzwilliam, and to your great surprise they both pay a visit to you at the parsonage shortly after arriving. Colonel Fitzwilliam is about thirty, not handsome, but in person and address most truly the gentleman. You are struck by the great difference between the two gentlemen; while Colonel Fitzwilliam enters into conversation with readiness and ease, his cousin sits without speaking to anybody. At length, however, Mr Darcy asks after the health of your family. You give the customary answer, and after a moment's pause, decide to ask him whether he has seen Jane in town. You know he has not, but wish to see how he reacts to the question: you are still convinced that Darcy and Miss Bingley have concealed from Mr Bingley their knowledge of Jane being in London. Darcy looks a little confused as he answers that he had not been so fortunate as to see Miss Bennet. You pursue the subject no further, and the gentlemen soon afterwards go away.

You receive an invitation to join the Rosings party for dinner on Easter Day and though you do not relish the prospect, you have little choice but to go. You are extremely grateful for the company of Colonel Fitzwilliam who comes to sit by you after dinner.

 The colonel's attentions are gratifying. Collect 10 CONFIDENCE POINTS.

The two of you converse with so much spirit and flow as to draw the attention of Mr Darcy, who, much as he did the night of Sir William's assembly, soon and repeatedly turns his eyes towards you, this time, however, with a look of curiosity.

Exciting Darcy's curiosity is likewise gratifying. Collect a further 10 CONFIDENCE POINTS.

The colonel asks you to play the pianoforte, and as you are halfway through your first song, Mr Darcy moves towards the pianoforte and stations himself so as to command a full view of you. You see what he is doing and with an arch smile you turn to him and say, 'You mean to frighten me, Mr Darcy, by coming in all this state to hear me? But I will not be alarmed though I do not play as well as some.'

'I shall not say that you are mistaken,' he replies, 'because you could not really believe me to entertain any design of alarming you; and I have had the pleasure of your acquaintance long enough to know that you find great enjoyment in occasionally professing opinions which in fact are not your own.'

You laugh heartily at this picture of yourself and are provoked to retaliate. You do so by relating to Colonel Fitzwilliam how Mr Darcy only danced four out of twelve dances at the ball where you first met, though more than one young lady was sitting down in want of a partner.

'I had not at that time the honour of knowing any lady in the assembly beyond my own party,' Mr Darcy defends himself.

 You sharpen your tongue and attempt, for the third time, to pierce his Shield of Pride. The fact that you've failed on two previous occasions clearly hasn't dulled your determination quite as much as it ought.

'True,' you reply, 'and nobody can ever be introduced in a ballroom.'

 It's a reasonable start. He ripostes:

'I certainly have not the talent which some people possess of conversing easily with those I have never seen before,' he continues. 'I cannot catch their tone of conversation, or appear interested in their concerns, as I often see done.'

 He's appealing to your feminine compassion. Will you be moved?

'My fingers,' you argue, with no compassion for his social ineptitude, 'do not move over this instrument in the masterly manner which I see so many women's do. But then I have always supposed it to be my own fault – because I would not take the trouble of practising.'

 No, apparently not.

You are interrupted by Lady Catherine, who is jealous of Mr Darcy's attention.

You're not just being modest; you really do play the piano remarkably ill. Answer the following question correctly and you could win some much needed musical talent.

What's the difference between a piano and a pianoforte?

Is it

a) A pianoforte makes a stronger sound than a piano: 'forte' being the Italian word for 'strong'.

Or

b) There is no difference. Pianoforte just sounds better.

If you think the answer is a), turn to page 197.

If you think the answer is b), turn to page 224.

You are only a fortnight from beginning your northern tour when a letter arrives from your aunt Gardiner, which at once delays its commencement and curtails its extent. Mr Gardiner's business obliges you to give up the Lakes and go no further northward than Derbyshire. The mention of Derbyshire brings forward many thoughts; it is impossible for you to see the word without thinking of Pemberley and its owner, Mr Darcy, whom you haven't seen since he gave you his most affecting letter at Rosings.

At length Mr and Mrs Gardiner appear at Longbourn and you set off the following morning in pursuit of novelty and amusement. You head first to the little town of Lambton, the site of Mrs Gardiner's former residence, which your aunt tells you is just five miles from Pemberley. Mrs Gardiner expresses an inclination to see Pemberley again and you are applied to for your approbation. You are distressed. The possibility of meeting Mr Darcy while viewing the place instantly occurs and you blush at the very idea. It would be truly dreadful and you think it better to speak openly to your aunt than to run such a risk. Understanding your concern, Mrs Gardiner asks the chambermaid whether the family is down for the summer, and a most welcome negative follows.

Collect 10 bonus FORTUNE POINTS.

With your fears allayed, you are at leisure to admit to yourself that you are indeed curious to see the house. You have heard stories connected to the place from both Darcy and Wickham, and moreover, cannot help wondering what kind of establishment

Mr Darcy keeps. When the subject is revived you can readily say, with a proper air of indifference, that you have not really any dislike to the scheme.

To Pemberley, therefore, you are to go.

Congratulations! You have completed Stage Three.

You show no signs of making a happy and prudent match any time soon, however. Take a long, hard look at yourself. It's not a pretty picture, but whose fault is that?

Proceed to Stage Four on page 251.

The rest of the evening at Rosings passes away pleasantly enough, and you spend most of your time engaged in conversation with the colonel.

The following morning, you are sitting by yourself and writing to Jane, when you are startled by a knock at the front door. The housemaid opens it and in a few moments, to your very great surprise Mr Darcy, and Mr Darcy only, enters the room.

 You curse your unlucky stars.

 They still do not appreciate being cursed.

 You lose 10 FORTUNE POINTS. When will you learn?

He too seems astonished on finding you alone: he had understood all the ladies to be within. You both sit down, and seem in danger of sinking into total silence. It is absolutely necessary, therefore, to think of something to say. The first thing that comes to mind are your suspicions concerning his part in Bingley's departure from Netherfield, and as your feelings of resentment against him rise up in you, you cannot help exclaiming abruptly, 'How very suddenly you all quitted Netherfield last November, Mr Darcy! I think I have understood that Mr Bingley has not much idea of ever returning to Netherfield again?'

You are curious to see what he has to say on the subject.

'Yes,' replies Darcy, 'I should not be surprised if he were to give it up as soon as any eligible property becomes available.'

You make no answer. You are afraid of talking longer of his

friend lest you should overcome the boundaries of decorum and accuse him outright of ruining your sister's happiness.

 You are exercising uncharacteristic levels of restraint. Collect 10 INTELLIGENCE POINTS.

Since you have nothing else to say, you are now determined to leave the trouble of finding a subject to him.

He takes the hint, and soon begins by remarking how agreeable it must be for Charlotte to be settled within so easy a distance of her family and friends. You know very well that Charlotte would not consider herself *near* her family at half this distance away and argue as much to Mr Darcy. Quite unexpectedly, he draws his chair a little towards you, and says, '*You* cannot have a right to such a very strong local attachment. *You* cannot have been always at Longbourn.'

You are surprised. You meant only that Charlotte would consider the cost of travelling such a distance to be too great to visit home regularly, and were not implying that she has any kind of provincial attachment to the village itself. You wonder why he should think you worldlier than Charlotte.

 He does, however, and your CONFIDENCE increases. Collect 10 CONFIDENCE POINTS.

On seeing your surprise, Mr Darcy appears to experience some change of feeling. He draws back his chair, takes a newspaper from the table, and, glancing over it, says, in a colder voice, 'Are you pleased with Kent?'

A short dialogue on the subject of the country ensues, and he soon afterwards quits the house. Your mind is disturbed by his confusing and contrary behaviour. 'What can he mean by it?' you ask yourself, until you grow so frustrated that you vow to waste no more time thinking unnecessarily about a man for whom you care very little indeed.

Mr Darcy clearly thinks you are well travelled, but he couldn't be more wrong. That could all change, however, if you answer the following question correctly!

Which is nearer to Longbourn?

Is it

a) Bath, or *b) Brighton*

If you think the answer is a), turn to page 198.

If you think the answer is b), turn to page 225.

You are proud to be prejudiced. You'll never learn from your mistakes because as far as you're concerned, you never make them.

 You are extremely sure of yourself. Collect 200 CONFIDENCE POINTS!

 You are however, farcically deluded. Deduct 200 INTELLIGENCE POINTS and add 'Farcically Deluded' to your list of FAILINGS.

Continue on page 194.

You refuse to take the letter and hastily turn back towards the parsonage. On your way you are surprised to see Colonel Fitzwilliam coming towards you on the very same path. You do your best to compose yourself, and are preparing to speak on some trivial matter when he saves you the trouble by beginning the conversation himself. 'In vain have I struggled,' says he, taking your hand. 'It will not do. My feelings will not be repressed. You must allow me to tell you how ardently I admire and love you.'

'Pardon?' you say, quite taken aback.

'In vain have I struggled,' he repeats. 'It will not do. My feelings will not be repressed. You must allow me to tell you how ardently I admire and love you.'

'Yes,' you say, in some surprise, 'I thought that's what you said.'

Good gracious, you think. Two proposals in as many days! You hardly know what to say. And from two separate members of the Darcy family! It's a wonder they didn't confer first, you think, before recollecting that the situation demands your attention and the colonel is, this very moment, anxiously awaiting your response.

The colonel wants to marry you.

If you think this would be an excellent way to get revenge on Mr Darcy, turn to page 148 to accept his proposal.

If you would rather work for your bread than marry any member of the Darcy family,[23] *turn to page 200 to politely refuse his offer.*

After this bewildering visit from Mr Darcy, he and his cousin find a reason to walk to the parsonage almost every day. It is clear that Colonel Fitzwilliam visits you because he has pleasure in your society, but why Mr Darcy comes so often to the parsonage it is more difficult to understand. Charlotte thinks he must be in love with you and watches him carefully. Whilst he certainly looks at you a great deal, however, the expression of that look is disputable: sometimes it seems nothing but absence of mind.

 Love/absence of mind – they're easily confused.

More than once in your ramble within the park do you unexpectedly meet Mr Darcy. To prevent its ever happening again, you take care to inform him at first that it is a favourite haunt of yours. How it could occur a second time, therefore, is very odd! Yet it does, and even a third.

 Deduct 10 INTELLIGENCE POINTS for not walking somewhere else.

You are engaged one day, as you walk, in re-perusing Jane's last letter when you are surprised not by Mr Darcy, but Colonel Fitzwilliam. You are always pleased to see him, and you walk together towards the parsonage. He and his cousin are to leave Kent on Saturday to visit Miss Darcy of whom, you learn, they are joint guardians. You are happy to tell him that you have heard a great deal of praise of her from Miss Bingley.

Although Colonel Fitzwilliam is not well acquainted with that lady, he knows of her brother through Mr Darcy and has reason to believe Mr Bingley much indebted to Darcy. You learn from the colonel that on their journey to Rosings, Mr Darcy congratulated himself on having lately saved a friend from the inconveniences of a most imprudent marriage. The colonel is sure his cousin must have meant Mr Bingley. Though you have long suspected it, you can hardly believe what you have heard. Shock, anger and disbelief overwhelm you. The colour rises in your cheeks.

'Did Mr Darcy give you his reasons for this interference?' you say, struggling to conceal your agitation.

'I understood that there were some very strong objections against the lady,' he replies.

Your heart swells with indignation.

'I do not see what right Mr Darcy had to decide on the propriety of his friend's inclination,' you exclaim with passion, but recollecting yourself you abruptly change the conversation and talk on indifferent matters till you reach the parsonage.

You shut yourself in the drawing room where you can think without interruption of all that you have heard, and the agitation and tears which the subject occasion bring on a violent headache. It grows so much worse towards the evening that, adding to your unwillingness to see Mr Darcy, it determines you not to venture to Rosings, where you and your party are engaged to spend the evening. When the others are gone you re-examine all the letters which Jane has written since your being in Kent, and Mr Darcy's shameful boast of what misery he has been able to inflict gives you a keener sense of your sister's sufferings.

*You are going out of your way to make yourself even more
miserable than you already are. Deduct 10 INTELLIGENCE POINTS.*

You are thinking of Mr Darcy with anger and resentment
when you are suddenly roused by the sound of the doorbell. To
your utter amazement, you see Mr Darcy walk into the room.
You can hardly believe your misfortune.

 Deduct 20 FORTUNE POINTS.

Never have you been more vexed to see him. In a hurried
manner he immediately begins an enquiry after your health,
imputing his visit to a desire to hear that your headache is better.
He is the last person you could wish to see at this moment and
you answer him with cold civility. He sits down for a few
moments, and then getting up, walks about the room. You are
furious with him for what he has done, and furious with him for
calling on you in this manner. Though you are surprised by his
pacing about the room, you say not a word. You can think of no
one with whom you could wish to converse less, and have not the
slightest inclination to ease his discomfort by finding a subject
upon which to talk. After an awkward silence of several minutes,
he comes towards you in an agitated manner, and thus begins:
'In vain have I struggled. It will not do. My feelings will not be
repressed. You must allow me to tell you how ardently I admire
and love you.'

Your astonishment is beyond expression. You stare, colour,
doubt, and are silent. You really are too shocked for words. This
he considers sufficient encouragement; and the avowal of all
that he feels, and has long felt for you, immediately follows. He
speaks well; but there are feelings besides those of the heart to

be detailed: his sense of your inferiority – of its being a degradation – of the family obstacles which have, until this moment, prevented him from making his feelings known to you, are dwelt on with warmth.

 Charming.

Your resentment rises. You try, however, to compose yourself so as to answer him with patience when he is through cataloguing your faults. He concludes by representing to you the strength of that attachment which, in spite of all his endeavours, he has found impossible to conquer; and by expressing his hope that it will now be rewarded by your acceptance of his hand.

To accept Mr Darcy's proposal, turn to page 191. He might not be particularly eloquent, but this is an offer you cannot refuse given your family circumstances. At least you'll be rich!

To refuse his offer, turn to page 172. You'd rather die an old maid than marry Mr Darcy.

You decide not to divulge Wickham's character to anyone else, and Jane at last is persuaded that there is no need to expose him since he will soon be gone from the neighbourhood. The tumult of your mind is allayed by this conversation, but still you dare not relate the other half of Mr Darcy's letter. On being settled at home, you are now at leisure to observe the real state of your sister's spirits and you see that she is not happy and still cherishes a very tender affection for Bingley. Though part of you earnestly wishes to, you cannot explain to Jane how sincerely she had been valued by Mr Bingley for fear of causing her further hurt by reviving hopes which can have little hope now of ever being realized. You are sorry for your sister, and do all that is in your power to revive her spirits and divert her attention away from any melancholy reflections on the past.

The first week of your return is soon gone and the second begins, announcing the last of the regiment's stay in Meryton. Lydia and Kitty regret it heartily, but the gloom of *Lydia's* prospect is shortly cleared away when she receives an invitation from Mrs Forster, the wife of the colonel of the regiment, to accompany her to Brighton. You wonder what you did to deserve this.

 Deduct 40 FORTUNE POINTS.

You consider the invitation the death warrant of all possibility of common sense for Lydia, and cannot help secretly advising your father not to let her go. Your father sees that your whole heart is in the subject, and affectionately takes your hand, and says in reply to your entreaty, 'My love, we shall have no peace at Longbourn if Lydia does not go to Brighton. Let her go, then. Colonel Forster is a sensible man, and will keep her out of any real mischief; and she is luckily too poor to be an object of prey to anybody.'

 You have no influence whatsoever.

With this answer you are forced to be content; but your own opinion continues the same, and you leave him disappointed and sorry.

 Add 'Lack of Influence' to your list of FAILINGS.

You see Mr Wickham one last time before he leaves Meryton. Upon his enquiry as to how you passed your time at Hunsford, you mention Colonel Fitzwilliam's and Mr Darcy's having both spent three weeks at Rosings. He asks you how you liked the colonel and you can tell from his manner that he expects you to join him once again in an abuse of the Darcy family. You cannot be drawn in this time, however. Instead, you drop a hint to Wickham that suggests his lies have been exposed when you say, 'The colonel's manners are very different from his cousin's, but I think Mr Darcy improves on acquaintance.'

Wickham's alarm appears in a heightened complexion and agitated look and when you part it is with a mutual desire of never meeting again.

Lydia leaves for Brighton early the next morning and you rejoice over Wickham's and the militia's departure. Peace settles on Longbourn once again, and you resume your usual daily routines.

The following day you decide to take a walk.

To visit your aunt Philips in Meryton, turn to page 245.

To call on the Lucases, turn to page 203.

You see that Mr Darcy has no doubt of a favourable answer. He *speaks* of apprehension and anxiety, but in his countenance you read smug security which only exasperates you further. That he should have taken the trouble to outline all his most insulting objections to you combined with your knowledge of his part in separating Jane and Bingley makes you angrier than you have perhaps ever before been in your life. When he ceases, you feel the colour rising in your cheeks, and you answer him by saying, 'In such cases as this, it is, I believe, the established mode to express a sense of obligation for the sentiments avowed, and if I could *feel* gratitude, I would now thank you. But I cannot – I have never desired your good opinion, and you have certainly bestowed it most unwillingly. I am sorry to have occasioned pain to anyone. It has been most unconsciously done, however, and I hope will be of short duration.'

Mr Darcy's surprise is evident.

 Could this be it? Could you FINALLY have pierced his insufferable Shield of Pride?

His complexion becomes pale with anger, and the disturbance of his mind is visible in every feature.

'And this,' says he, struggling for composure, 'is all the reply which I am to have the honour of expecting! I might, perhaps, wish to be informed why, with so little *endeavour* at civility, I am thus rejected. But it is of small importance.'

 Clearly, his Pride is still intact.

'I might as well enquire,' you reply, incensed at his unfaltering pride, 'why with so evident a design of offending and insulting me, you chose to tell me that you liked me against your will, against your reason, and even against your character? And even if my own feelings had not decided against you, do you think that any consideration would tempt me to accept the man who has been the means of ruining, perhaps for ever, the happiness of a most beloved sister?'

 That ought to wound him.

As you pronounce these words Mr Darcy changes colour. The emotion is short, however.

 But clearly doesn't.

He listens without attempting to interrupt you while you challenge him to deny that he has been the principal, if not the only, means of dividing Jane and Bingley from each other and involving them both in misery of the acutest kind. You pause, and see that he is listening with an air which proves him wholly unmoved by any feeling of remorse. He even looks at you with a smile of affected incredulity which only infuriates you further.

'Can you deny that you have done it?' you ask him again.

With assumed tranquillity he admits to being the agent of your sister's despair, adding, 'I rejoice in my success. Towards *him* I have been kinder than towards myself.'

The colour rises in your cheeks.

 It's time to use your secret weapon.

'But it is not merely this affair,' you continue, 'on which my dislike is founded. Your character was unfolded in the recital which I received many months ago from Mr Wickham. On this subject, what can you have to say?'

'You take an eager interest in that gentleman's concerns,' says Darcy, in a less tranquil tone, and with a heightened colour.

At last, a reaction. Angry though you are, exciting Mr Darcy's jealousy gives you a little thrill. Collect 10 bonus CONFIDENCE POINTS.

'Who that knows what his misfortunes have been, can help feeling an interest in him?' you continue. 'You have reduced him to his present state of poverty and deprived him of the best years of his life, of an independence which was no less his due than his desert!'

'And this,' cries Darcy, as he walks with quick steps across the room, 'is your opinion of me! My faults, according to this calculation, are heavy indeed! But perhaps,' he adds, stopping in his walk, and turning towards you, 'these offences might have been overlooked, had not your pride been hurt by my honest confession of the scruples that had long prevented my forming any serious design. But disguise of every sort is my abhorrence. Could you expect me to rejoice in the inferiority of your connections? To congratulate myself on the hope of relations, whose condition in life is so decidedly beneath my own?'

You are incensed, and feel yourself growing angrier by the moment. You try your utmost to speak with composure when you reply, saying, 'You are mistaken, Mr Darcy, if you suppose that the mode of your declaration affected me in any other way, than as it spared me the concern which I might have felt in refusing you, had you behaved in a more gentlemanlike manner.'

You see him start at this.

FINALLY. Using your own Pride as your weapon, you have pierced Darcy's Shield of Pride. He might be a gentleman, but Darcy's notion of gentility is deeply flawed and you alone have dared to challenge it. Collect 100 FORTUNE POINTS, 100 INTELLIGENCE POINTS and 100 CONFIDENCE POINTS as your reward. You deserve them. Whether you can hang on to them is another matter...

Darcy says nothing, and you continue, 'You could not have made me the offer of your hand in any possible way that would have tempted me to accept it.'

Again his astonishment is obvious; and he looks at you with an expression of mingled incredulity and mortification. You cannot regret it, and with renewed energy you go on, 'Your arrogance, your conceit, and your selfish disdain of the feelings of others are such that I had not known you a month before I felt that you were the last man in the world whom I could ever be prevailed on to marry.'

Okay, stop now. Don't rub it in.

'You have said quite enough, madam,' says Darcy, with forced civility. 'I perfectly comprehend your feelings, and have now only to be ashamed of what my own have been. Forgive me for having taken up so much of your time, and accept my best wishes for your health and happiness.'

And with these words he hastily leaves the room, his spirits clearly disturbed, and the next moment you hear him open the front door and quit the house.

The tumult of your mind is painfully great. Overwhelmed by feeling, you sit down and cry for half an hour. That you should receive an offer of marriage from Mr Darcy, that he should have been in love with you for so many months – so much in love as to wish to marry you in spite of all the objections which have made him prevent his friend's marrying your sister – is almost incredible! Despite yourself, you cannot help feeling that it is gratifying to have unconsciously inspired so strong an affection.

You can't help it. Your CONFIDENCE *increases. Collect 20 points.*

But his pride, his abominable pride, his shameless avowal of what he has done with respect to Jane, his unpardonable assurance in acknowledging his cruelty to Mr Wickham, soon overcomes the gratification momentarily excited by the consideration of his attachment. You continue in very agitating reflections till the sound of the Collinses returning hurries you away to your room.

You awake the next morning to the same thoughts and meditations which at length closed your eyes. You proceed directly to your favourite walk and after walking two or three times along the same part of the lane, Mr Darcy suddenly appears. 'I have been walking in the grove some time in the hope of meeting you,' says he, holding out a letter. 'Will you do me the honour of reading this?'

For a moment, you are not sure what to do. You have no desire to be insulted any further, and nothing he could possibly say could now induce you to accept his proposal, or forgive him for ruining the happiness of both Jane and Wickham.

To accept the letter regardless, turn to page 183.

To refuse it, turn to page 164.

You have absolutely no appreciation of the picturesque whatsoever and are entirely unworthy of a trip to the Lakes.

 Deduct 100 INTELLIGENCE POINTS and add 'Absolutely no Appreciation of the Picturesque' to your list of FAILINGS.

No wonder you're still single.

Continue on page 151.

―――――>●<―――――

You agree to go with your father to the evening assembly at Hartfield Hall, a large estate owned by your father's old acquaintance, Mr Woodhouse, who is in Hertfordshire for the summer months. Though Mr Woodhouse and his daughter used to live at Hartfield permanently, they have for many years now been living in London, and until recently the estate has been let to an admiral and his wife.[24] You are therefore not well acquainted with them yourself and have never been to Hartfield before. Consequently, though you regret missing the Westons' picnic, you look forward to your evening at Hartfield with a degree of curiosity. In addition, since they are such close neighbours, you have every expectation of seeing Mr Knightley there and so anticipate a most pleasant evening.

When Saturday arrives you make your journey to Hartfield with your father and not long after entering the drawing room, are pleased to see a few familiar faces. Mr Knightley, as you suspected, is present, as is Mr Frank Churchill.

You foresee a pleasant evening. Collect 10 FORTUNE POINTS.

Sir William Lucas and his wife are also there, though not with Maria who has been taken ill with a violent headache. You are sorry to hear it, and when Mr Churchill expresses his own concern for her health with such sincerity, you cannot help smiling, though you are a little surprised. 'There is hope for Maria yet,' you think to yourself.

Across the room you spy a handsome young woman whom you instantly guess to be Mr Woodhouse's daughter Emma.[25] You have heard a good deal about her, but do not remember ever having met her. From what you have heard, Emma Woodhouse is clever, talented and accomplished; and you anticipate the introduction to such an impressive woman with a small degree of trepidation. At the moment you spy her she is in receipt, perhaps a little less than willingly, of the most assiduous attentions of a local clergyman. Wherever she moves in the room he follows and is always at her elbow, obtruding his happy countenance on her notice, and solicitously addressing her upon every occasion. His name, you learn, is Mr Elton, and you overhear him admiring the many drawings of hers which adorn the walls of Hartfield with so much zeal and so little knowledge as instantly confirms to you that he is very much in love with Miss Woodhouse. When she sits down on the sofa with a friend a few moments later, he immediately draws up and without an invitation sits himself between them. Perhaps having witnessed it themselves, Miss Woodhouse's father and yours choose this moment to introduce the two of you, and Miss Woodhouse seems truly grateful for the interruption. Your fathers leave you to become better acquainted and you have not been talking for long when you are joined by Mr Knightley and Mr Churchill.

'Mr Knightley!' cries Emma in rapturous delight, immediately turning away from you and addressing herself almost exclusively to him, as if there were no one else present in the room. 'How I have missed you! And how glad I am that you have returned to the neighbourhood. But I have been in Hertfordshire above a month now, Mr Knightley, and my father and I have hardly seen you at Hartfield. You do not visit us as often as you were wont, I think.'

'I'm sorry to hear you say it,' replies Mr Knightley, seemingly a little taken aback at this reproach.

'Come, come. You cannot deny it!' she goes on. 'And yet I

think you have found your way to Longbourn more than once, have you not?'

She is smiling, but Miss Woodhouse's tone of playfulness is not altogether convincing.

'Mr Bennet is an esteemed friend of mine,' replies Mr Knightley; 'and since your father is likewise well acquainted with Mr Bennet,' he goes on, catching Miss Woodhouse's playfully reproachful tone, 'I can only say that I am surprised that I do not see *you* there more often.'

She chooses to ignore this last comment.

'I do not think it is just Mr Bennet that you go for, though, is it?' she replies, turning to smile at you, though not altogether warmly.

You open your mouth to speak but are prevented by Miss Woodhouse suddenly exclaiming, 'And you too, Mr Churchill! I expected to see more of you at Hartfield after our first introduction. Mr Weston gave me such expectations of you, that I must confess I am disappointed not to have seen more of you.'

Mr Churchill, quite taken aback, seems a little lost for words, which is no matter for Miss Woodhouse seemingly desires no reply and instead turns abruptly to you and exclaims gaily, 'But Miss Bennet! I wonder that we have not become better acquainted before this evening.'

She takes your arm in hers and continues in a warm tone of friendliness, 'And when I heard that our Mr Knightley was so often at your house, I thought we really *had* to meet before any further loss of time. But come,' she says, drawing you away from Mr Knightley and Mr Churchill, 'I have somebody I wish you to meet. These gentlemen will excuse us, I am sure,' she concludes, smiling beguilingly at them.

You are surprised indeed, and a little confused.

Though she is behaving strangely, you are still keen to make a good impression on Miss Woodhouse. This is where your ability to bluff really comes into play. How did you do in the Society Test? Which Society Type did people think YOU were? Turn to the relevant page to see what you say next!

Not 'Riche' At All? Turn to page 199.

Nouveau Riche? Turn to page 221.

Old Money? Turn to page 249.

You take the letter, and with a slight bow, Darcy turns again into the plantation and is soon out of sight.

It is dated from Rosings, at eight o'clock in the morning, and begins as follows:

'Be not alarmed, madam, on receiving this letter, by the apprehension of its containing any repetition of those sentiments or renewal of those offers which were last night so disgusting to you. You must pardon the freedom with which I demand your attention; your feelings, I know, will bestow it unwillingly, but I demand it of your justice.'

With no expectation of pleasure, but with the strongest curiosity, you read on.

'Two offences of a very different nature, and by no means of equal magnitude, you last night laid to my charge and I must endeavour now to explain my actions and motives.'

You learn that he had seen that Bingley preferred your sister but it was not till the Netherfield dance that he had any apprehension of it being a serious attachment. It was Sir William's comments that made him aware that their marriage was considered a certain event by the whole neighbourhood. He observed Bingley closely and could perceive that his partiality was beyond any that he had witnessed in him before, but though Jane received his attentions with pleasure she did not seem to invite them by any participation of sentiment. He did not believe her to be indifferent because he wished it, he believed it on impartial conviction. Here you cannot help from exclaiming out loud – you do not believe a word of it. How could he have mistaken Jane's reticence for *indifference*? Impossible. He goes on to say that there were 'other causes of repugnance'.

Ouch.

You smart at his use of the word. Your mother's lineage, he tells you, though objectionable, was nothing in comparison of that total want of propriety so frequently betrayed by her, by your flirtatious younger sisters, and occasionally even by your father.

Oh dear.

You are overcome with mortification.

Deduct 50 CONFIDENCE POINTS.

Your mortification quickly turns to anger, however. What right has he to insult you, and your entire family, in such a way? Though you cannot entirely deny the truth of what he says, you hardly think it necessary for the purposes of his letter for him to express his feelings so openly. Darcy goes on to apologize for offending you and consoles you by praising you and Jane for having conducted yourselves so as to avoid any share of the censure which the rest of your family has earned.

Your deflated CONFIDENCE creeps up by 10 points.

His compliment is not unfelt, though it can do little to atone for his affront on the rest of your family. With nerves greatly agitated, you read on. Miss Bingley's uneasiness had been equally excited by the situation, and agreeing that no time should be lost, they joined Bingley in London. Darcy pointed out the evils of such a choice, described them earnestly, and assured him of Jane's indifference. You actually begin to shake with indignation. Bingley's natural modesty meant it was easy for Darcy to convince him he had been deceived, and to persuade him against returning to Hertfordshire was the work of a moment. Darcy does not blame himself for this much but regrets concealing Jane's being in town, admitting that it may have been beneath him.

 How magnanimous of him.

He has nothing more to say on the matter and no further apology to offer. You are incredulous and outraged. His belief of Jane's indifference you resolve to be entirely false; and his account of the real, the worst objections to the match, make you too angry to have any wish of doing him justice. He expresses no regret for what he has done, which satisfies you; his style is not penitent, but haughty. It is all pride and insolence.

 As usual.

He then proceeds to defend himself against your second, more weighty accusation, of having injured Mr Wickham. Here, you are sure, he can have nothing to say to excuse his behaviour. You harden your resolve against him and read on. He sets out the circumstances of their early years together, much of which you have already learnt from Wickham. Mr Darcy's father supported Wickham through school, and afterwards at Cambridge, and had the highest opinion of him.

 No news here. Your CONFIDENCE inches up by another 10 points.

185

After their fathers died, Wickham wrote to Darcy to ask for money in lieu of preferment since he had resolved against taking orders and had some idea of studying the law. Darcy rather wished than believed him to be sincere, but acceded to his proposal despite his reservation. Wickham resigned all claim to assistance in the Church in return for three thousand pounds. All connection between them seemed then to dissolve, and Darcy thought too ill of him to invite him to Pemberley.

Wickham lived in town but law was just a pretence and being now free from restraint, his life was one of idleness and dissipation. You can hardly believe it, and attribute Darcy's account to his prejudice against him, and jealousy of his father's affection for Wickham.

Once again, deduct 10 INTELLIGENCE POINTS for continuing in your Wilful Prejudice.

For about three years Darcy heard little of Wickham; but on the decease of the incumbent of the living which had been designed for him, he wrote to Darcy asking for it. His circumstances were exceedingly bad, he had found the law a most unprofitable study, and was now absolutely resolved on being ordained. Darcy refused to comply with this entreaty, and resisted every repetition of it. You are once more furious at Darcy when you recall his having boasted, while you were at Netherfield, of the implacability of his resentments. 'Here is evidence enough!' you say to yourself, before reading on. After this period every appearance of acquaintance was dropped until last summer when Wickham again most painfully obtruded on Darcy's notice.

Your CONFIDENCE begins to falter. Deduct 20 points.

His sister Miss Darcy, who is ten years his junior, was taken from school a year ago to an establishment in London and last summer went with Mrs Younge, the woman who presided over it, to Ramsgate. Thither Mr Wickham also went, having learnt of their plans from Mrs Younge herself, with whom he had a prior acquaintance, and in whose character Darcy had been most unhappily deceived. By her connivance and aid he so far recommended himself to Georgiana that she believed herself in love and consented to an elopement. You are shocked beyond words. Mr Darcy joined them unexpectedly a day or two before the intended elopement, and she was unable to conceal it from him. Astonishment, apprehension, and even horror oppress you.

Oh dear. Your judgement really is breathtakingly poor. Add 'Breathtakingly Poor Judge of Character' to your list of FAILINGS.

You read on. Mr Wickham left the place immediately and Mrs Younge was removed from her charge. Mr Darcy invites you to consult Colonel Fitzwilliam if you need further testimony and concludes by saying:

'I will only add, God bless you. Fitzwilliam Darcy.'

You wish to discredit the letter entirely, and when you have gone through the whole, you put it hastily away, protesting that you will not regard it, that you will never look at it again. But it will not do: in half a minute the letter is unfolded again. The extravagance and general profligacy with which he charges Mr Wickham exceedingly shocks you; the more so, as you can bring no proof of its injustice. Of his former way of life nothing had been known in Hertfordshire but what he told himself. Aside from his affable company, you try to recollect some instance of goodness, some distinguished trait of integrity or benevolence, that might rescue him from the attacks of Mr Darcy; but no such recollection befriends you.

 Oh dear, oh dear. Deduct another 50 CONFIDENCE POINTS.

You remember everything that had passed in conversation between Wickham and yourself, in your first evening at Mr Philips's: he boasted of having no fear of seeing Mr Darcy – yet he avoided the Netherfield ball the very next week. You remember also that, before the Netherfield party had quitted the country, he told his story to no one but yourself; but that after their removal it was everywhere discussed.

Every lingering struggle in Wickham's favour grows fainter and fainter.

 Strike 'Mr Wickham' from your list of SUPERIOR CONNECTIONS and add him to your list of INFERIOR CONNECTIONS.

Proud and repulsive though Mr Darcy's manners are, you have never, in the whole course of your acquaintance – an acquaintance which has latterly brought you much together – seen anything that betrayed him to be unprincipled or unjust; seen anything that spoke him of irreligious or immoral habits.

You grow absolutely ashamed of yourself.

 And rightly so.

Of neither Darcy nor Wickham can you think without feeling that you have been blind, partial, prejudiced, absurd.

> *Add 'Blind', 'Partial', 'Prejudiced' and 'Absurd' to your list of* FAILINGS.

'How despicably have I acted!' you cry; 'I, who have prided myself on my discernment! Till this moment I never knew myself.'

> *Admitting this is the first step towards Self-Awareness.*

> *Congratulations!*

> *With Self-Awareness comes mortification.*

> *Bad luck.*

Your thoughts turn to Jane – at least Mr Darcy's explanation *there* was very insufficient. You read it again but your heart sinks as you realize how widely different is the effect of a second perusal. You cannot deny the justice of his description of Jane and feel that Jane's feelings, though fervent, are little displayed, and that there is a constant complacency in her air and manner not often united with great sensibility.

After wandering along the lane for two hours, giving way to every variety of thought, fatigue, and a recollection of your long absence, makes you at length return home.

Mr Darcy's letter has affected you, there's no doubt about that, but how profoundly? Just how stubborn is your pride? Are you ready to renounce your trademark prejudice? Take the following test to find out!

You have just learnt that everything you thought you knew was wrong.

Do you

a) *Vow never to make the same mistakes again; beg for forgiveness; punish yourself again and again for all you have done and thought; turn to your Bible for comfort and advice henceforward; and dedicate the rest of your life to your sin's atonement.*

b) *Vow never to make the same mistakes again but eventually learn to forgive yourself.*

c) *Vow never to make the mistake of thinking you were wrong ever again. What came over you? You are always right! Are you going to let some man tell you what to think? You think not.*

If you answered a), turn to page 201.

If you answered b), turn to page 247.

If you answered c), turn to page 163.

With all the good grace you can manage in the circumstances, you accept Mr Darcy.

Mr Collins is shocked indeed to hear the news, and his first thought is of Lady Catherine. You know he will never forgive you for displeasing her but you comfort yourself with the knowledge that you'll soon be rich beyond your wildest dreams and will not have to see Mr Collins above twice a year.

If Mr Collins's shock is great, it is nothing next to that of your nearest relations. Jane is greatly fearful for your happiness, your father hardly less so, and your *mother*, for once, is entirely lost for words.

Your wedding is an intimate affair; with Darcy so offended by the inferiority of your connections, it could hardly be otherwise. After you have taken leave of your family in sombre spirits, you remove with your husband to Pemberley and settle into your new life.

Mr Darcy is civil to you when he is with you, but his duties on the estate are many, and frequently draw him from you. Not that you care much; it is a relief to be spared the necessity of making conversation. Mr Darcy has yet to learn how to converse with you on an easy footing and more often than not either inadvertently insults you, or is silent.

Without even the companionship of an affectionate husband to divert you, there is little for you to do at Pemberley. You are therefore forced to pass the long hours of the day reading your way through the many books in your extensive library, or walking about the estate and the surrounding countryside.

It is on one of these many walks, about a month after your marriage, that you meet the farmer responsible for the farm attached to Pemberley. He is a very plain man, remarkably plain, but that is nothing compared with his entire want of gentility.[26] You wonder that Mr Darcy could have employed such a man, when he manages to find fault with a gentleman like your father. At first it astonishes you that a man could be so very clownish, so totally without air, but as your acquaintance grows, you find yourself increasingly attracted to the farmer. The situation at home shows no signs of improving and when Mr Darcy isn't working, he spends more time reading than talking to you. Your resentment increases, and the more Mr Darcy neglects you, the less guilt you feel for seeking the society of Mr Robert Martin. Your morning walks take you past his farm more frequently and your conversations grow longer. You are astonished and delighted to discover that not only is he literate, but he actually takes a keen interest in books. He even goes so far as to make you some recommendations, lending you *The Vicar of Wakefield*, for which you are most grateful, and which you are careful to conceal from the notice of your husband.

At last, unable to bear the stifling atmosphere at home any longer, you engage in a full and passionate affair with Mr Martin. It soon becomes public knowledge and you and Mr Martin are banished in disgrace, forever cut off from society, and are forced to spend the rest of your days in squalid lodgings in Portsmouth[27] until the misery of your situation ruptures your love entirely and you hate each other with all the ardent passion with which you once loved. Wretched and grief-stricken, you take your life in an agony of despair and regret.

THE END

Your mission was to marry both prudently and for love, remember? You hated Darcy, and an affair with his farmer was hardly prudent, was it?

You have FAILED.

Mr Darcy and Colonel Fitzwilliam leave Rosings the very next morning. Until the time comes for you to leave Hunsford, you spend your days taking solitary walks in which you indulge in all the delight of unpleasant recollections.

You are going out of your way to make yourself even more miserable than you already are. Again. Deduct 10 INTELLIGENCE POINTS.

At last you say your farewells and begin your journey which will take you first to London to collect Jane. Within four hours of your leaving Hunsford you reach your uncle and aunt Gardiner's house, where Jane has been staying. You stay the night before journeying on to Longbourn with your sister. You arrive in good time, and Kitty and Lydia give you news of the neighbourhood. You learn with some satisfaction that the militia is to leave Meryton in a fortnight for Brighton and the only other news of interest is that the woman to whom Wickham has been paying his attentions has left the country for good. 'Lucky for her' you think to yourself.

You have not been many hours at home before you find that Lydia has a plan for the whole family to follow the militia to Brighton for a holiday.

Dear God.

The thought of your entire family exposing itself to further ridicule and censure in Brighton is almost too much to bear. You cannot think of a worse idea.

Darcy was right; nobody in your family has any sense whatso-
ever. Deduct 20 CONFIDENCE POINTS. Your CONFIDENCE really
is at an all-time low right now. Thinking about it decreases
your CONFIDENCE even more. Unlucky. Deduct another 20
points.

Your mother thinks it an excellent scheme; your father, thankfully, does not agree. He has not the smallest intention of yielding; but his answers are at the same time so vague and equivocal, that your mother has not yet despaired of succeeding at last.

Your impatience to acquaint Jane with what happened can no longer be overcome. Resolving to suppress every particular in which she is concerned, the next time you are alone you relate to her the chief of the scene between Mr Darcy and yourself. Her astonishment at his proposal and shock concerning what his letter had to tell of Wickham are great. Jane feels that it is your duty to make your knowledge public and expose Wickham as the fraud he really is. You are not so sure that it is a good idea: Mr Darcy has not authorized you to make any of his communication public, and the details relating to his sister were meant to be kept as much as possible to yourself. And in any case, Wickham will soon be gone and therefore it cannot really make much of a difference to anybody in Meryton whether or not they know his true character.

If you think you should go public, but omit the details about
Georgiana, turn to page 208.

If you decide to keep it to yourself, turn to page 169.

Congratulations! Your appreciation of the picturesque is outstanding.

 Add 'Outstanding Appreciation of the Picturesque' to your list of ACCOMPLISHMENTS and collect 100 bonus FORTUNE POINTS.

You are entirely worthy of a trip to the Lakes, and it's only a wonder that you've never been before.

Continue on page 151.

Wrong.

Deduct 200 INTELLIGENCE POINTS for making such a STUPID mistake.

That was a trick question. 'Piano' is simply an abbreviation of 'pianoforte'. The fact that you got this question wrong proves just how little time you've spent playing one.

You continue to be a talentless musician.

Continue on page 160.

Wrong!

You have no sense of geography beyond your own backyard.

 Deduct 100 INTELLIGENCE POINTS.

If you'd ever been to Brighton, you'd know that it is closer to Longbourn than Bath.

 You remain very poorly travelled.

Continue on page 165.

NOT 'RICHE' AT ALL

You tell her how much you admire her drawings, confess that you cannot draw yourself, that you never had a governess, and that in fact you have no education whatsoever.

 Miss Woodhouse holds you in the highest contempt. Deduct 100 INTELLIGENCE POINTS.

Continue on page 228.

You politely refuse the colonel's kind offer, and make your way back to the parsonage.

Charming though you are, you never receive another offer of marriage as long as you live. There was never any guarantee that you would. Apparently, that was your last chance.

 Who knew?

THE END

You have failed. Too bad.

Have some pride. Nobody's going to want to marry you if you carry on like that.

Deduct 100 INTELLIGENCE POINTS.

Continue on page 194.

NOUVEAU RICHE

You run the risk of people thinking you made your money from trade, but if you pretend to like the countryside a little less, you might get away with being thought of as nothing worse than nouveau riche.

 Collect 50 FORTUNE POINTS and try to eat more potatoes.

Continue on page 211.

You call on the Lucases and learn from them that one of your acquaintances is returning to the area tomorrow following a long spell abroad. After your recent trials, you could not be more delighted to hear it. Mr Knightley has been a friend to your family for many years and is greatly esteemed by your father, with whom he has spent many an evening playing backgammon. He is a firm favourite of *yours* too, and you are very pleased that he is returning now, when you are trying to forget Darcy's letter.[28] Both handsome and agreeable, Mr Knightley more often than not has a cheerful manner. Though he is quick to remind you of your faults, you have learnt to bear it well, and respect his candour. He is perhaps the wrong side of five and thirty, but has vigour, if not youth, to recommend him, and is lively in spirit. Now that Charlotte is no longer at home, you feel that Maria would also benefit from his society at this time, and having grown fond of her since the time you spent together at Hunsford, you promise to take her to visit Mr Knightley often. You are only too happy to help where the inconvenience to yourself is so very small.

How generous of you.

Mr Knightley lives about a mile from Longbourn, and is the owner of a handsome estate by the name of Donwell Abbey. You visit him often, usually with Maria, and often with Jane too. You and Mr Knightley have much to discuss after such a long period of separation and you are grateful to have somebody with which to talk over your present fears and anxieties over Lydia's holiday in Brighton. Mr Knightley expresses surprise that your father let her go in the first place, and is a little concerned himself knowing what he does of Lydia's character, but he encourages you not to worry yourself unduly about it. He turns the conversation towards happier subjects and you both express your pleasure at the recent marriage between an old childhood friend of yours, Miss Taylor, and one of Mr Knightley's oldest acquaintances, Mr Weston. The new Mrs Weston and her husband have moved to Randalls, a handsome property close to Donwell Abbey. You are both very happy for them and agree to call on them together at the earliest opportunity. The visit is made the following morning and you learn that they are expecting a visit from Mr Weston's son from a prior marriage, Mr Frank Churchill.

 A new arrival. Good news. Collect 10 bonus FORTUNE POINTS.

You are confused as to why Mr Weston's son does not share his surname, but you learn that Frank has been raised by his wealthy uncle and aunt on his mother's side of the family, and since he is their heir, he has adopted their surname.

Mrs Weston confesses to you that she is a little nervous about meeting him, and hopes she will be accepted. You are extremely curious to see him yourself, not least because Mr and Mrs Weston seem to have very great hopes of the two of you getting along very well, and seem very anxious to make the introduction.

 Things are looking up. Collect another 10 FORTUNE POINTS.

Your interest in Mr Churchill, and your desire to meet him, naturally increases. There is a great deal of excited talk of Frank

Churchill in Meryton, and everyone seems eager for his appearance. Mr Knightley alone seems indifferent to the prospect of his arrival, and cannot understand why the whole neighbourhood should be so excited, or upon what evidence they are basing their opinion that he is such an 'impressive man of honour' etc.

'If I find him conversable,' says he one morning, 'I shall be glad of his acquaintance; but if he is only a chattering coxcomb, he will not occupy much of my time or thoughts.'

You are amused by Mr Knightley's tone, and accuse him, in good humour, of being prejudiced against Mr Churchill.

'Prejudiced!' he cries with a degree of vexation. 'I am not prejudiced. He is a person I never think of from one month's end to another.'

You cannot imagine why he should be angry, and, finding it all very funny, you tease him about his prejudice against Mr Churchill from this time forward. It's only fair. Mr Knightley picks up on all *your* faults, after all.

Frank Churchill does not appear at the time appointed for his much anticipated visit and everybody's hopes are disappointed.

Oh dear. Deduct 10 bonus FORTUNE POINTS.

Mrs Weston's anxieties about meeting him increase but her husband assures her that Frank's aunt and uncle Churchill have more than likely exercised their rights over a dependent nephew and that Frank will come at last. It seems that the Churchills never approved of Mr Weston and it would not surprise him if they had deliberately caused a delay. Mrs Weston's fears are appeased, but Mr Knightley is quick to condemn Frank for the disrespect he has shown towards his new stepmother by not coming, and seems to feel justified in his first unfavourable surmise as to Frank's character. Once again you are somewhat taken aback by the violence of Mr Knightley's reaction against Mr Churchill and cannot help having a good laugh about it. You really cannot comprehend why he should be so angry towards him before even making his acquaintance.

The Churchills do not approve of Mr Weston largely because he made his money in trade. To the landed gentry this is the most heinous sin of all. Your father is a gentleman, but who is your mother? Could you bluff your way in society and pass for a real gentlewoman? Why not take the **Society Test** to find out which Social Type people would think YOU are. Would they be fooled? Find out! Now!

You are at an important and exclusive society event, and somebody asks you to describe yourself.

Which of the following would *you* say in response?

a) You live in the countryside and prefer it to town; consider potatoes something of a delicacy; like to wash the choice china with your own hands; love walking and wear unfashionable but practical pattens to negotiate the muddy village lanes.[29]

CONTINUED

CONTINUED

b) *You live in the countryside but also enjoy life in town; you have potatoes fairly regularly; you never wash dishes yourself; you love walking but only go out in fashionable nankin half-boots.*[30]

c) *You live in the countryside but can't stand it and long for the superior society of London; you eat potatoes for every meal, even breakfast; you would rather die than wash a dish yourself; and only travel by carriage, preferably a barouche or landau.*[31] *Exercise is for peasants.*

If you answered a), turn to page 246.

If you answered b), turn to page 202.

If you answered c), turn to page 227.

You decide to make public the true nature of Wickham's character and share all details made known to you, excepting those relating to his attempted seduction of Georgiana. The people of Meryton are greatly shocked, but when they have finally come round to the truth they begin to imagine that they always thought there was something suspicious about him. Wickham is dismissed from his regiment and quits the county in disgrace. Kitty and Lydia vow never to forgive you.

Which means they talk to you less; a happy consequence.
Collect 10 INTELLIGENCE POINTS.

It is a long time before you hear any news of him, but some months later he returns to the neighbourhood and calls at Longbourn to tell you that, thanks to you, he has seen the error of his ways, seen the light, and found God. He is once again determined to make the Church his profession, and this time he really means it. He has renounced his life of sin and has dedicated the rest of his life to atoning for it. He has come to Longbourn expressly to thank you for your part in his revelation; without you, he would still be in the hands of the devil. He seems really to be in the grip of religious fervour, and talks in such a strange manner that you begin to feel that you preferred him as a sinner. But he is never to return to his old ways, and moreover, wishes to thank you for showing him the path of righteousness by marrying you.

You are quite taken aback. When you decided to expose Wickham, little did you think it would lead to this. Though he claims to have undergone a complete transformation, you remain sceptical and extremely wary of him. You thank him for his kind offer to marry you, and assure him that he has done his duty to God in asking you, and is now free to return home with a clear conscience. But you have underestimated Mr Wickham, who is deadly serious in his intentions. He will marry you if it's the last thing he does.

You only have yourself to blame. Deduct 50 INTELLIGENCE POINTS for ever having exposed him.

And so begins Mr Wickham's campaign to win your heart. He lets a cottage close to Longbourn and visits you every day; he copies out sections of the Bible that he thinks you will find instructive; he picks you wild flowers and informs you of their healing properties; he insists on accompanying you on all your walks, whether you like it or not; and he submits to the ridicule directed at him by every single member of your family except Jane, just to show his humility before God and your good self.

After many, many months, you can take it no more. At last convinced of his transformation, and knowing that he will never give up his mission to make you his wife until you agree to marry him, you do so. There was no chance of anybody else succeeding while Mr Wickham was there to ward them off. Wickham is so delighted when you tell him the news, that he spontaneously breaks out into song, and serenades you with his favourite celebratory hymn.

You are married before the month is out, much to the disgust of every member of your family except Jane: she, at least, is grateful that you have put an end to Wickham's relentless and intrusive wooing.

You remove to London so that Wickham can complete his religious studies and have not been there above a week when you discover a most shocking truth. The whole of the last year and a half has been an elaborate and merciless scheme on Wickham's part to exact revenge on you for having so cruelly exposed him. He doesn't love you and never has, has nothing but scorn for the Church, and wanted only to devastate and ruin you until you lost the will to live. Though the past months have been long and difficult, and he thought of giving up many times, he declares that it has all been worth it for the pleasure of seeing your hope, your faith in humanity, and your whole perception of reality entirely crushed. While you weep on the floor in an agony of despair, he burns his copy of the Bible before setting out to victoriously gallivant around London, whoring and gaming to his heart's content, caught up in a delicious ecstasy of impropriety and sin. You never recover from your distress and die shortly afterwards.

THE END

> *Yes. You guessed it. You have failed.*

———————

At long last Mr Churchill arrives and the Westons call on you at Longbourn to make the introduction. You are sitting with Maria Lucas and Jane when they arrive and you are all extremely pleased to finally meet Mr Churchill. Your mother and other sisters are quick to join you when they hear who has come to visit. You do not think too much has been said in his praise. He is a *very* good-looking gentleman and has an air of real elegance. His manner and address are good and you like him immediately. When he has gone, you are all generous in his praise.

'He is the most handsome man I ever saw in my life!' exclaims Maria.

Your mother declares him better looking than Mr Bingley, and Kitty pronounces him more handsome even than Mr Wickham. You cannot deny it, and though Jane does not agree that he is more handsome than Mr Bingley, she admits that he is superior to Mr Wickham in looks. You both hope that he will prove to be likewise superior in *character*. You are all very pleased to have a new face in the neighbourhood, particularly after the departure of the militia, and you feel that Mr Churchill will be of some assistance in helping you to take your mind off Mr Darcy and his letter, which you still take out and reread from time to time; each time more ashamed at what your own behaviour has been.

Deduct 10 INTELLIGENCE POINTS for YET AGAIN going out of your way to make yourself even more miserable than you already are.

Mr Churchill calls on you the next day and you accompany him and his stepmother on a tour of Meryton. He is warm and genuine in his praise of all that he sees. After walking together so long, and thinking so much alike, you feel yourself so well acquainted with him, that you can hardly believe it to be only your second meeting.

🌃 *Collect 10 bonus FORTUNE POINTS.*

Mrs Weston sees it all with pleasure and more than once do you catch her smiling expressively as you and Mr Churchill converse.

———————

Mr Knightley's society brings you once more into contact with Mrs and Miss Bates. Mrs Bates is a very old lady, who lives modestly with her single daughter. Miss Bates boasts neither youth, beauty nor cleverness, and yet she is a happy woman, and a woman whom no one names without goodwill. You used to visit them frequently, but have lately been very remiss in your attentions. Following a lecture from Mr Knightley on your duties to those less fortunate than yourself, your conscience is pricked.

🌃 *Add 'Reprehensibly Remiss in Duties to Those Less Fortunate' to your list of FAILINGS.*

You resolve to call on them with Jane and Maria the very next day. Miss Bates has a niece, Jane Fairfax, who was taken into the care of a Colonel Campbell and his family following the death of her own parents. Miss Bates talks of Jane Fairfax almost as much as Mr Collins talks of Lady Catherine de Bourgh and every letter from her is read by her aunt forty times over. When you pay your visit you are welcomed most cordially and gratefully by Miss Bates who is almost ready to overpower you with care and kindness, thanks for your visit, enquiries after your parents' health, cheerful communications about her own mother's, and sweet-cake from the sideboard before suddenly exclaiming that she has this very morning had an unexpected letter from Miss Fairfax. Your heart sinks, but your politeness is at hand directly, to say, with smiling interest, 'Have you heard from Miss Fairfax so lately? I am extremely happy. I hope she is well?'

 Add 'Ability to Feign Interest in the Utterly Boring' to your list of ACCOMPLISHMENTS. *You'll need that when you're married.*

Miss Bates assures you that she is and eagerly hunts for the letter. The unexpected news from this particular epistle is that Miss Fairfax is to visit her aunt, and will arrive this very weekend. You are very curious to see the esteemed Jane Fairfax, though after hearing so much in her praise, do not altogether look forward to the meeting with pleasure.

 How incredibly ungenerous of you. Forfeit 20 FORTUNE POINTS.

Your sister is more generous, and expresses her pleasure at the prospect of making Miss Fairfax's acquaintance very soon, and promises to call on her often.

When Jane Fairfax appears you are forced to admit that she is both uncommonly handsome and very well accomplished. Your mother declares her remarkably plain and no match for your own dear Jane, whom she hopes will soon catch the heart of Mr Churchill since Mr Bingley shows no signs of returning. She cares not that you have taken a liking to him yourself – you are the least favourite of all her daughters. You put your prejudice against Miss Fairfax aside and make her acquaintance but upon getting to know her better, however, you revert to your former dislike; you find her cold and reserved and you cannot forgive her for it.

 Add 'Jealousy' to your list of FAILINGS.

You are curious to know Mr Churchill's opinion of her and he is united with you in condemnation of her reserve, which cannot but please you. Mr Knightley seems to admire her greatly, however, and when you are slow to join him in his praise of her, he accuses you of being prejudiced against Miss Fairfax, just as you accused him of being prejudiced against Mr Churchill. You cannot help but laugh when it is represented to you in this way, but still you cannot teach yourself to like Miss Fairfax, despite your best efforts.

 Your best efforts, are they? Really?

Mr Knightley reproaches you for not paying your attentions to her as you ought, and reminds you that her situation is much less fortunate than your own.

 Deduct 10 FORTUNE POINTS for once again being reprehensibly remiss in your attentions to those less fortunate than yourself. Thankfully, Mr Knightley is always close at hand to point out your many mistakes.

Miss Fairfax might have been raised as a gentleman's daughter, but no provisions were made for her adult life and consequently she will soon be forced to take work as a governess. In the light of this, you feel the justness of Mr Knightley's reproach and vow to be more attentive to Miss Fairfax henceforward.

 But aren't. Deduct 10 FORTUNE POINTS for making empty promises.

You have been spending a great deal of time with Frank Churchill lately and more than once do you hear Mr Knightley complain of Frank's showing off. You respect Mr Knightley's opinion, and fearing that you could be making the same error of judgement you made with Wickham, are concerned that he does not think highly of Mr Churchill. When you ask him to give more by way of explanation for his feelings of antipathy towards Mr Churchill, however, he has little to say in reply. You therefore continue to think well of Mr Churchill, who does not disappoint you.

Until, that is, the following day when you hear that he is gone off to London merely to have his hair cut.

 Your sense of your own judgement is shaken. Again. Deduct 10 CONFIDENCE POINTS.

You would not have expected such frivolous behaviour from him and begin to fear that he really is another Wickham. Mr Knightley is at Longbourn when the circumstance is told and for the moment he is silent, but you hear him almost immediately afterwards say to himself over a newspaper he holds in his hand, 'Hum! Just the trifling, silly fellow I took him for.' Though you cannot agree that it is reflective of Frank's character in general, you privately concede to Jane that evening that going to London merely to have his hair cut was indeed a less than sensible thing to do. For this reason, when Frank returns from London you are wary of him. As a precaution against making another error of judgement you decide to exercise more reserve in his company than you have shown hitherto.

You would have earned 10 INTELLIGENCE POINTS for this had you not criticized Jane Fairfax for being reserved. Serves you right.

He soon wins you round with his intelligence and sharp sense of humour, however, and over the ensuing weeks you warm to him once again and your attachment grows steadily. Shortly after his return from London, Jane Fairfax receives an anonymous gift of a pianoforte, and both you and Frank are united in your suspicions that it must have come from her guardian's married son. You are sure that he must be in love with Jane Fairfax, and you both marvel at the scandal of it all.

It's not like you to indulge in such frivolous and unsubstantiated gossip. Deduct 10 INTELLIGENCE POINTS.

From this time forward, you spend many evenings and days together with Frank Churchill and you both derive great pleasure from one another's company. You are particularly pleased that he is always so ready to join you in criticizing Miss Fairfax, and he assures you kindly one evening that though she is superior to you in her piano playing, you definitely outshine her at dancing.

This is untrue. Deduct 10 FORTUNE POINTS for believing it.

You cannot entirely approve of his impropriety in saying it, but nevertheless such compliments cannot help but gratify your vanity.

Collect 10 CONFIDENCE POINTS.

Vanity is STILL a sin.

Deduct 10 FORTUNE POINTS. When will you learn?

You are just beginning to form a sincere and serious attachment to Mr Churchill, when Frank receives a letter from his uncle urging his return home on account of his aunt having been taken extremely ill. You are sorely disappointed. Frank Churchill comes to take leave of you and seems on the point of confessing to you his love when he is most untimely interrupted by his father.

Deduct 20 FORTUNE POINTS.

Both gentlemen shortly take leave and you are very disappointed to see Mr Churchill go. When he has departed, Jane, concerned for your happiness, wants to know the strength of your feelings for Mr Churchill.

'Well, Jane,' you reply with humour, 'from this sensation of listlessness, weariness, stupidity, this disinclination to sit down and employ myself, and this feeling of everything's being dull and insipid about the house, I can only conclude that I must be in love.'

Though you are joking, there is more than a little truth in what you say. Though you think of him a great deal just after he has gone, however, and form a thousand imaginary schemes for the progress and close of your attachment, the conclusion of every imaginary declaration on his side is that you refuse him. When you become aware of this, it strikes you that you cannot be very much in love after all.

Oh well. Easy come, easy go.

This seems to you of all things the most perverse, and you begin to wonder whether you will ever be happily settled when your feelings are so fickle. You were sincerely attached to Mr Wickham at one time, only to discover that you were sorely deceived in his character. And here is a man in every way perfect for you, and yet you cannot force your feelings into love. You really believe that you could be happy with Mr Churchill if you could only love him, but there is nothing you can do about it. You grow quite frustrated with yourself, and then endeavour to shake off your sombre mood by laughing at the ironic misfortune of the situation.

There's nothing you can't laugh off, is there?

Maria seems particularly melancholy following Mr Churchill's departure and you begin to wonder if she is not in love with him herself. Your suspicions are further aroused when during the course of some trivial chat about marriage Maria says in a very serious tone, 'I shall never marry.' You look up at her and see her meaningful and troubled expression. It seems to you that Maria is indeed in love with Mr Churchill, but somehow considers him too superior for her. It is true that she has no fortune to speak of; lacks wit, and on occasion intelligence too; is certainly not handsome – but in all other respects you do not consider her too far beneath Mr Churchill for a marriage to be possible.

'Is your resolution, or rather your expectation of never marrying, the result of an idea that the person whom you might prefer would be too greatly your superior to think of you?' you query her gently.

'Oh! Miss Elizabeth,' she cries. 'Believe me I have not the presumption to suppose – indeed I am not so mad. But it is a pleasure to me to admire him at a distance.'

You are touched by her modesty and resolve to praise her many merits when next in the company of Mr Churchill.

 How charitable of you. Collect 10 bonus FORTUNE POINTS. Her sister was happy with one of your rejects, so why shouldn't she be?

Though he has never paid her any particular attention, you do not consider the case entirely hopeless. The greatest obstacle that stands in her way, as far as you see it, is that Mr Churchill is presently in love with *you*.

Before long Mr Churchill is able to return, owing to his aunt and uncle moving south to take advantage of the better weather. When he pays you his first visit, you perceive a change in his addresses: he has fallen out of love.

 Deduct 10 CONFIDENCE POINTS. The fact that you've fallen out of love with him too makes no difference whatsoever. It's never nice, is it?

'At least Maria stands a better chance now!' you laugh to yourself.

There you go again, laughing it off.

A few days later, you and Jane receive an invitation from the Westons to join them for a day trip and picnic at a picturesque location a few miles from Meryton. Just moments later, your father receives an evening invitation for the same date from an old acquaintance staying near Donwell Abbey. It seems that the invitation has been explicitly extended to include you, and your father is anxious not to disappoint his friend. Owing to the distance between both parties, and the fact that your father will be using the carriage, you are only able to accept one invitation.

To accept the Westons' picnic invitation, turn to page 230.

To accept the evening invitation, turn to page 179.

Nouveau Riche

You tell her how much you admire her drawings, make out as if you draw yourself, pretend you were taught by a governess, and ask her how much she paid for her pencils.

 Miss Woodhouse thinks you extremely vulgar. Deduct 50 INTELLIGENCE POINTS.

Continue on page 228.

400 *OR ABOVE*

You and Mr Knightley are united in marriage at the earliest opportunity, to the delight of all your friends and family. Even Mr Collins sends you a grudging letter of congratulations. You remove to Donwell Abbey and settle into your new life. Being close to your family and friends is a great comfort, and your father often comes to spend the evening, and you have the pleasure of being in the company of your two favourite gentlemen in the whole world. You are happy for a while but it soon becomes apparent to Mr Knightley that you are smarter than he gave you credit for and you often find yourselves in dispute. Your arguments increase in frequency and seriousness until it gets so unbearable that you spend your days at opposite ends of the house just to avoid each other. You remain married, but most unhappily.

THE END

> *You have failed to complete your mission. A high*
> INTELLIGENCE SCORE *is not always a good thing: to come*
> *with a well-informed mind is to come with an inability of*
> *administering to the vanity of others, which a sensible*
> *person would always wish to avoid. A woman, especially,*
> *if she has the misfortune of knowing anything, should*
> *conceal it as well as she can.*[32] *You are a LOSER.*

You have an extremely basic appreciation of the picturesque. You don't really deserve to look on the majestic beauty of the Lakes, but might get away with it if you point admiringly to withered oaks and use adjectives such as 'bold' and 'rugged' from time to time.

Continue on page 151.

Correct.

'Piano' is simply an abbreviation of 'pianoforte'. Obviously.

 You can now play the piano reasonably well. Add 'Reasonable Piano-Playing Skills' to your list of ACCOMPLISHMENTS. It might not be much, but it's a vast improvement. Yes. You're that bad at the piano.

Continue on page 160.

Correct!

Brighton is, indeed, closer to Longbourn than Bath.

 Collect 100 INTELLIGENCE POINTS.

 You may now add 'Once Spent the Day at Weston-super-Mare' to your list of ACCOMPLISHMENTS. Nobody can accuse YOU of local attachment.

Continue on page 165.

You refuse Mr Knightley and he is devastated. At his age, by the time he's gotten over you, he'll be way past it. He gives up Donwell and goes to live in Antigua.[33] What he does there is anybody's guess; you never hear from him again.

No longer in his company, you forget Mr Knightley, and turn your thoughts instead towards your forthcoming tour of the lakes with your aunt and uncle Gardiner. You are more in need of a break now than you have ever been.

Continue on page 158.

Old Money

Well done! Everyone will think you are Old Money and invite you to join them in scoffing at those who made their money from trade. Your attitudes reflect your great wealth and natural good taste that have been passed down from generation to generation.

Or they would if you weren't bluffing, and really were rich. But you are not.

 Deduct 50 Fortune points for having to bluff in the first place. Now you have even more need to bluff. It's a vicious circle.

Continue on page 211.

Miss Woodhouse takes you directly to meet Mr Elton, and after hastily making the introduction, leaves the two of you to get better acquainted. She returns to Mr Knightley and Mr Churchill, and taking them each by the arm, leads them to another part of the room.

There can be no mistaking her behaviour. You have been most shockingly snubbed. Deduct 50 CONFIDENCE POINTS.

It is some moments before you can recover from the surprise and give your full attention to Mr Elton, who is wasting no time in trying to make himself agreeable to you, and is at this moment urging you to take a seat lest you should tire yourself by standing for too long. He goes on to pay you such assiduous attention and so many compliments that you can hardly believe he is the same man you saw, just moments ago, devotedly following Miss Woodhouse wherever she went – he appears to have turned his attentions from Emma to you with the same ease and rapidity with which Mr Collins diverted his from Jane to yourself.

Mr Elton clearly has no sense, and after you have been stuck with him for above two hours, you manage to shake him off and go in search of your father. You find him without much difficulty, and urge him to take you home as soon as possible. He is surprised, and reluctant to leave, but at last assents to order the carriage. By this time Mr Elton has found you again, and is at your elbow, entreating you to stay and expressing his concern for your safety on your journey. You assure him that there is no danger at all, that the weather is as fine as it could be, and the distance but small. You hurry to the carriage with Mr Elton trailing behind you, entreating, imploring you to take just one more glass of punch with him before you leave. Your father finds him highly amusing, and is totally insensible of the distress which Mr Elton's very public, and quite unwanted, attentions are giving you.

You climb into the carriage and shut the door behind you before Mr Elton can follow, and order the driver to be off at once. Mr Elton is really unwilling to let you go, however, and gallantly stands in the path of your vehicle, flinging his arms open wide, and demanding the driver stop immediately. He gives the horses such a fright as he does so that they at once rear up in a great panic and as their hooves come crashing back down on the gravel in a frenzy of confusion, Mr Elton is untimely trampled to death. The general public blames you for his death and you are tried and imprisoned for the crime of remorselessly killing a man of the cloth.

THE END

It was a miscarriage of justice, but nobody could care less. You have failed to complete your mission.

You accept the Westons' invitation and look forward to it with pleasure. Maria has likewise been invited and seems particularly keen to make an impression, going as far as to ask your advice on what she should wear. You put it all down to her growing attachment to Mr Frank Churchill, who will also be in attendance, and give her your best advice as to which of her gowns shows her off to best advantage whilst still being suitable for an afternoon party. When Saturday comes the weather is very hot indeed, and you are in high spirits. You set off for your picnic in anticipation of a very pleasant day and you, Mr Knightley, the Bateses, Jane Fairfax, your sister Jane, Frank, the Westons and the Lucases reach your destination in time for a short walk before picnicking.

Frank Churchill is talkative and gay over lunch, making you his first object. After chatting for some time amongst companions almost silent due to the oppressive heat, Frank leans towards you and whispers, 'Our companions are excessively stupid. What shall we do to rouse them?' He evidently thinks of something at once as he suddenly turns towards the general company and embarrasses you by making a loud announcement.

'Ladies and gentlemen,' says he, 'I am ordered by Miss Bennet to say that she demands, by way of entertainment, from each of you either one thing very clever, be it prose or verse, original or repeated, or two things moderately clever, or three things very dull indeed, and she engages to laugh heartily at them all.'

Though you find him amusing, you wish he had not said it all in your name. From your sister Jane's alarmed and concerned expression you see that she, at least, knows you would never have said such a thing yourself.

 Unlike everyone else present, who now thinks you are incredibly rude.

You do your best to hide a blush.

'Oh! Very well,' exclaims Jane Fairfax's loquacious aunt, Miss Bates, 'then I need not be uneasy. "Three things very dull indeed." That will just do for me, you know. I shall be sure to say three dull things as soon as ever I open my mouth, shan't I?' she says, looking round with the most good-humoured dependence on everybody's assent. 'Do not you all think I shall?'

You are amused by her light-hearted satirical self-awareness, and, inspired by Frank's audaciousness, cannot resist a retort.

'Ah! ma'am, but there may be a difficulty,' you say with a smile. 'Pardon me, but you will be limited as to number – only three at once.'

Everyone is silent and you instantly regret what you have said.

 Whoops.

Miss Bates, deceived by the mock ceremony of your manner, does not immediately catch your meaning; but, when it bursts on her, due to her good nature it cannot anger, though a slight blush shows that it pains her.

'Ah! Well – to be sure. Yes, I see what she means,' she says, turning to Mr Knightley, 'and I will try to hold my tongue. I must make myself very disagreeable, or she would not have said such a thing to an old friend.'

Mr Knightley is very grave, Lady Lucas excuses herself by

saying she has no pleasure from such diversions, and Jane Fairfax offers her aunt her arm.

'Now, ma'am,' says she to Miss Bates, 'shall we join Lady Lucas?'

They walk off, followed in half a minute by Mr Knightley who takes your sister Jane with him, though she is reluctant to leave you at such a time. You wish that you had not been so influenced by Mr Churchill's insouciance, but earnestly hope that your joke will soon be forgotten.

 It won't. Deduct 10 FORTUNE POINTS.

You are left to the flattery of Mr Churchill and the conversation of Maria, which all at once you find insipid and extremely dull. The appearance of the servants looking out for you to give notice of the carriages is, therefore, a joyful sight. While waiting for the carriage, you suddenly find Mr Knightley by your side. He seems to have something particular to say to you, and looks around as if to see that no one is near before speaking. You fear he has come to criticize you, and your fears are not unjust. He prefaces his speech by saying that he cannot see you acting wrong without a remonstrance, and that he claims the privilege of speaking to you as he used to do.

'How could you be so unfeeling to Miss Bates?' he continues. 'How could you be so insolent in your wit to a woman of her character, age, and situation?'

You are mortified.

 Deduct 100 CONFIDENCE POINTS.

You blush, are sorry, but try to laugh it off.

Laughing it off isn't going to work this time. Deduct 10 FORTUNE POINTS.

'Nay, how could I help saying what I did?' you reply. 'Nobody could have helped it. It was not so very bad. I dare say she did not understand me.'

You rather hope than believe it to be true.

'I assure you she did. She felt your full meaning. She has talked of it since. I wish you could have heard how she talked of it – with what candour and generosity – honouring your forbearance in being able to pay her such attentions as she was forever receiving from yourself, when her society must be so irksome.'

You feel all the force of his criticism.

Deduct 50 CONFIDENCE POINTS.

But still you feel you must defend yourself. You were wrong to say it, but you did not say anything but what everybody present was thinking. You endeavour to shake off the gravity of the situation by saying that though there is not a better creature in the world, even Mr Knightley must allow that what is good and what is ridiculous are most unfortunately blended in her. But Mr Knightley is not so easily appeased.

'They are blended,' says he, 'I acknowledge; and, were she prosperous, I could allow much for the occasional prevalence of the ridiculous over the good. But consider her situation, and how unequal it is to your own. She is poor; she has sunk from the comforts she was born to; and, if she lives to an old age, must probably sink more. Her situation should secure your compassion. It was badly done, indeed! To have you laugh at her, humble her – and before her niece, too.'

To have upset Miss Bates is bad enough, and you now regret it deeply, but Mr Knightley's disapprobation mortifies you beyond expression.

 Deduct a further 50 CONFIDENCE POINTS.

He seems actually disappointed in you, and you heartily wish you could do or say something that might do greater justice to his former high opinion of you. The carriage draws up and before you can speak again, he has handed you in. Never have you felt so agitated, mortified, grieved, at any circumstance in your life.

 You lose all remaining CONFIDENCE POINTS and must deduct 50 INTELLIGENCE POINTS for ever making such a stupid mistake in the first place.

You are most forcibly struck. The truth of his representation there is no denying. You feel it at your heart. How could you have been so brutal, so cruel to Miss Bates? How could you have exposed yourself to such ill opinion in anyone you value? Your spirits are dreadfully depressed.

The wretchedness of a scene at the picnic is in your thoughts the whole evening long and on Jane's advice, the following morning you pay a visit to the Bateses to make amends for your insulting blunder. Miss Fairfax does not leave her room, and though Miss Bates is polite, there is not the same cheerful volubility as before.

 If you had any CONFIDENCE POINTS left, you'd lose them here.

234

You feel the change deeply, and wish you could do something to show that you are sorry. A very friendly enquiry after Miss Fairfax, you hope, might lead the way to a return of old feelings. The touch seems immediate. Miss Bates thanks you for your kindness and you learn that Miss Fairfax has just accepted a position as governess to a family living at some distance from Meryton. To be forced by reduced circumstances to take a position as governess must be a hard lot indeed for one raised as highly as Miss Fairfax has been, and for the first time in your life you feel genuine compassion for her. You offer condolences to Miss Bates who will surely miss her society dearly.

You'll have to do a lot more than that if you want to be forgiven.

You return home to find that Mr Knightley and Maria have arrived during your absence. You are sure Mr Knightley has not forgiven you; his behaviour is not what it usually is. Time, you console yourself, will tell him that you ought to be friends again. While he stands as if meaning to go, your mother begins her enquiries.

'And how did you find my old friend and her daughter? Lizzy has been to call on the Bateses and Miss Fairfax, Mr Knightley. She is always so attentive to them,' she says, all smiling attention to Mr Knightley.

Your colour is heightened by this unjust praise; and with a smile, and shake of the head, which speaks much, you look at Mr Knightley. All that has passed of good in your feelings, however, are at once caught and honoured. He looks at you with a glow of regard. You are warmly gratified – and in another moment still more so, by a little movement of more than common friendliness on his part. He takes your hand, presses it, and certainly is on the point of carrying it to his lips when, from some fancy or other, he suddenly lets it go. Why he should feel such a scruple, why he should change his mind when it was all but done, you cannot perceive.

 It's better than nothing though. Collect 10 CONFIDENCE POINTS.

The intention, however, is indubitable; and you cannot but recall the attempt with great satisfaction. It speaks such perfect amity.

 Collect another 10 CONFIDENCE POINTS.

He tells you that he will be away visiting his brother in London for some days, and leaves immediately afterwards, in a haste which does not speak of perfect ease. You hope that when he returns, time will have eased all remaining tension between you.

Mr Churchill has been in London since the picnic, and the day following Mr Knightley's departure thither, Mrs Weston receives a letter from Frank giving the news of the death of his aunt. Frank is now free to do as he pleases and marry where he likes – a blessing for Maria – and you are delighted for him. Maria seems very happy to hear this latest news which only confirms your suspicions about her feelings for him. You have never seen him show any particular attention to her, however, but hope for her sake that he will begin to notice her now and see beyond her plain looks and appreciate the sweet-natured girl within. You vow once again to praise her many good qualities next time you speak with Mr Churchill. She deserves a good husband, and with youth on her side, you feel that with a little help she has a chance to make a better match than her sister Charlotte.

Not that your help's worth much. Still single yourself, aren't you?

Ten days following the death of Mrs Churchill you receive a visit from Mr Weston who is most out of sorts and entreats you to return with him to Randalls directly. You are greatly alarmed, and your mother has a fit of nerves. When you arrive at Randalls you find that Mrs Weston is quite as upset as her husband. You urge her to speak immediately. Her voice trembles and she cannot look you in the eye.

'Frank has been here this very morning, on a most extraordinary errand. It is impossible to express our surprise. He came to speak to his father on a subject – to announce an attachment...'

Mrs Weston stops to breathe. You think first of yourself, and then of Maria.

'More than an attachment, indeed,' resumes Mrs Weston; 'a positive engagement! What will you say – what will anybody say, when it is known that Frank Churchill and Miss Fairfax are engaged; nay, that they have been secretly engaged since last October, when, it appears, they met at Weymouth!'

You had no idea they had ever met before and almost jump with surprise.

'Jane Fairfax! You are not serious? You do not mean it?'

Mr Churchill has always been so disparaging of Miss Fairfax, and you wonder that you could have been so deceived. It suddenly strikes you that it must have been *Mr Churchill* who sent Jane the pianoforte, which he must have bought when he went to London and told everyone that he had gone merely for a haircut. You think with horror of your conversations with Frank about Miss Fairfax and are deeply ashamed of what your behaviour has been.

Again.

Mr and Mrs Weston are both most anxious for you, believing that you are in love with Frank yourself. It is with some difficulty that you are at last able to convince them that though you were at some time attached to Mr Frank Churchill, it has been many weeks since you have been able to think of him as anything but an amiable acquaintance. You wonder, however, how Miss Fairfax could have borne his attentions to you, and cannot but think ill of Frank for his behaviour towards you both.

'Poor Maria!' you think to yourself as you walk home. You call on her to give her the news and are quite surprised to discover that she has already heard it and does not appear to be in the least bit upset. You begin to wonder whether you have been mistaken in thinking her in love with Mr Churchill.

'I am pleased to see that you are not distressed by the news, Maria,' you say with a smile. 'I must confess that I thought you had formed an attachment to him yourself, and am pleased, in this case, to be proved wrong.'

How big of you.

'Me! In love with Mr Churchill!' exclaims Maria. 'How could you think such a thing? Never, never. I do not know who could ever look at him in the company of the *other*...'

It quickly becomes apparent that you were not mistaken in

thinking her in love, only in the object of her affections. You are confused. If Maria has not been in love with Mr Churchill then who *has* she been in love with? It is at this moment that a most distressing thought crosses your mind. You are suddenly struck with the awful possibility that she could mean Mr *Knightley*. It is suddenly absolutely necessary to have that thought contradicted.

'Maria!' you cry, before recollecting yourself. 'Let us understand each other now. Are you speaking of ... Mr Knightley?'

You almost dread her response. When she tells you that she is indeed talking of Mr Knightley, and thought you knew, your worst fears are confirmed. You assure her that you most certainly did not. Maria is standing at one of the windows and you turn around to look at her in consternation.

'And have you any idea of Mr Knightley's returning your affection?' you ask with trepidation.

'Yes,' replies Maria modestly, but not fearfully, 'I must say that I have.'

 You only have 20 CONFIDENCE POINTS to lose. Say goodbye to them now.

Your eyes are instantly withdrawn; and you sit silently meditating, in a fixed attitude, for a few minutes. It darts through you suddenly, with the speed of an arrow, that you love Mr Knightley. A thousand feelings rush on you at once and from this moment you are wretched indeed. Only when threatened with his loss, do you realize how much you love him.

 Deduct 50 INTELLIGENCE POINTS for not realizing it sooner.

Maria Lucas might think herself not unworthy of being exclusively and passionately loved by Mr Knightley, but *you* cannot. You remember how shocked he was by your behaviour to Miss Bates; how directly, how strongly he expressed himself to you on the subject. Not too strongly for the offence – but far, far too strongly to issue from love or indeed any feeling softer than upright justice and clear-sighted goodwill. He has always been awake to your faults and has shown no scruples in pointing them out to you; no, Mr Knightley could never be in love with *you*.

You have no CONFIDENCE POINTS left to lose. Deduct 50 FORTUNE POINTS instead.

The following day you take a walk about the garden to refresh your depressed spirits. You have only taken a few turns, when you see Mr Knightley passing through the garden door, and coming towards you. You did not even know he had returned from London. There is time only for the quickest arrangement of mind. You must be collected and calm. The 'How d'ye do's' are quiet and constrained on each side. You think he neither looks nor speaks cheerfully; and the first possible cause for it, suggested by your fears, is that he had perhaps communicated his plans to marry Maria to his brother while in London, and is pained by his unfavourable reaction.

You walk together. He is silent, and you cannot bear it long; something must be said. Trying to smile, you begin, 'You have some news to hear, now you are come back, that will rather surprise you.'

'Have I?' says he quietly, and looking at you. 'Of what nature?'

'The best nature in the world, Mr Knightley – a wedding,'

you say, hinting at what you are sure is to pass between him and Maria.

After waiting a moment, as if to be sure you intend to say no more, he replies, 'If you mean Miss Fairfax and Frank Churchill, I have heard that already.'

'How is it possible?' you exclaim, turning your glowing cheeks towards him; for while you speak, it occurs to you that he might have called at the Lucases on his way.

'I had a few lines on parish business from Mr Weston this morning, and at the end of them he gave me a brief account of what had happened.'

You are quite relieved.

 Collect 20 CONFIDENCE POINTS.

For a moment or two nothing is said. Suddenly you find your arm drawn within his, and pressed against his heart, and hear him thus saying, in a tone of great sensibility, speaking low, 'Time, my dearest Elizabeth, time will heal the wound.' Your arm is pressed again, as he continues in a more broken and subdued accent, and you just manage to catch the words '… indignation… Abominable scoundrel!'

You understand him; he believes you in love with Mr Churchill and therefore imagines you to be suffering at the news of his engagement to Miss Fairfax. Such tender consideration cannot help but give you a flutter of pleasure.

 Collect 50 CONFIDENCE POINTS.

As soon as you have recovered, you endeavour to assure him that you are not, and never have been, attached to Frank Churchill.

'My vanity was flattered, and I allowed his attentions, but I soon realized they were not serious. He has imposed on me, but he has not injured me. I have never been attached to him.'

 How many more times? Vanity is a sin. Deduct 40 FORTUNE POINTS. Add 'Shameless Vanity' to your list of FAILINGS. You won't be told again.

You hope for an answer here – for a few words to say that your conduct was at least intelligible; but he is silent; and, as far as you can judge, deep in thought.

'He is a most fortunate man!' he suddenly exclaims with energy. 'He meets – at a common *watering place* – with an infinitely superior young woman, gains her affection, treats her negligently and conceals his engagement from his aunt. Then, when his aunt conveniently dies, he makes the engagement public and everyone is eager to promote his happiness. He has used everybody ill – and they are all delighted to forgive him. He is a fortunate man indeed!'

'You speak as if you envied him,' is your nervous reply, fearing every moment a declaration of his love for Maria.

'And I do envy him, Elizabeth. In one respect he is the object of my envy.'

 Here goes...

You can say no more. You seem to be within half a sentence of Maria, and your immediate feeling is to avert the subject, if possible. Before you can speak, Mr Knightley startles you, by saying, 'You will not ask me what is the point of envy. You are determined, I see, to have no curiosity. You are wise – but *I*

cannot be wise. Elizabeth, I must tell what you will not ask, though I may wish it unsaid the next moment.'

You cannot bear to hear it.

'Then, don't speak it,' you exclaim eagerly. 'Take a little time, consider, do not commit yourself.'

'Thank you,' says he, in an accent of deep mortification, and not another syllable follows. You cannot bear to give him pain.

 But you have. Deduct 20 INTELLIGENCE POINTS.

He wishes to confide in you – perhaps to consult you; cost you what it will, you will listen. You apologize for stopping him ungraciously and assure him that he can speak to you openly on any subject 'as a friend'.

'As a friend!' repeats Mr Knightley. 'Elizabeth, I fear that word. But I have gone too far already for concealment. Elizabeth, tell me, as a friend then, have I no chance of ever succeeding?'

He stops in his earnestness to look the question, and the expression of his eyes overpowers you. He entreats you to give him an answer at once, and say 'No' if it is to be said. You can really say nothing; you are overwhelmed with emotion at this most extraordinary and unexpected turn of events.

 Collect 200 CONFIDENCE POINTS and 200 FORTUNE POINTS.

It seems to you that he is making a proposal, but you scarcely dare to hope that it is true.

'I cannot make speeches, Elizabeth,' he resumes, and in a tone of sincere, decided and intelligible tenderness. 'If I loved you less, I might be able to talk about it more. But you know what I am. You hear nothing but truth from me. I have blamed you, and lectured you, and you have borne it as no other woman in England would have borne it. Bear with the truths I would tell you now, dearest Elizabeth, as well as you have borne with them. The manner, perhaps, may have as little to recommend them.'

You cannot help laughing as you remember with tender reflection the many, many times Mr Knightley has chastised you.

 He really has chastised you a lot.

And all the while he loved you! It is most extraordinary.

'God knows,' he continues, 'I have been a very indifferent lover. But you understand me. Yes, you see, you understand my feelings – and will return them if you can. At present, I ask only to hear, once to hear your voice.'

> *Mr Knightley is making you a proposal of marriage.*
>
> *If you wish to accept the eligible Mr Knightley, you must first check your INTELLIGENCE SCORE.*
>
> *If it is 400 or above, turn to page 222.*
>
> *If it is below 400, turn to page 248.*
>
> *If you wish to refuse him, suddenly doubting whether you could truly be happy with a man who is almost twice your age and who might continue to 'blame' and 'lecture' you to the end of your days, turn to page 226. A leopard rarely changes his spots.*

You call on your aunt Philips, who talks of little but the departure of the militia and what a loss it is to the neighbourhood. You wish you had visited the Lucases.

The following weeks pass peacefully and uneventfully, and with little else to divert you, you turn your thoughts to your forthcoming tour to the Lakes.

Continue on page 158.

Not 'Riche' At All

Nobody will think YOUR family made their money from trade. Nobody will think your family has any money AT ALL.

 Deduct 100 Intelligence points for being so honest.

 Nevertheless you have the courage to risk the scorn and disdain of all those around you, which is as charming as it is foolish. Collect 50 bonus Fortune points.

Continue on page 211.

You have been prejudiced but are not too proud to admit it. You learn from your mistakes and learn your lesson well.

 Collect 200 INTELLIGENCE POINTS and 100 FORTUNE POINTS.

Continue on page 194.

BELOW 400

You marry Mr Knightley and remove to Donwell Abbey to settle into your new life. A short while after your wedding, you hear that Mr Darcy has married Miss Bingley and you feel a small pang of something like regret, though you chastise yourself for your foolish feelings. You put it from your mind as soon as possible and learn to be content with Mr Knightley.

THE END

Congratulations. You have completed your mission.

OLD MONEY

You tell her how much you admire her drawings, say they remind you of some of Constable's landscapes, tell her how excessively you like art, and pretend you have taken the Grand Tour.

 Everyone within earshot believes you are Old Money. Congratulations! Collect 100 FORTUNE POINTS.

 Miss Woodhouse is intimidated by your superior knowledge, and hates you all the more for it. Deduct 50 INTELLIGENCE POINTS.

Continue on page 228.

STAGE FOUR

S YOU DRIVE along, you watch for the first appearance of Pemberley with some perturbation; and when at length you arrive at the gate, your spirits are in a high flutter. You drive for some time through a beautiful wood stretching over a wide extent and you silently admire every remarkable spot and point of view. You soon see the house itself on the opposite side of a valley. It is a large, handsome stone building, standing well on rising ground, and backed by a ridge of high woody hills. You are delighted. You have never seen a place for which nature has done more, or where natural beauty has been so little counteracted by an awkward taste for artificial 'improvements'. After the pomp and honour of Rosings, you had rather expected to find Darcy's family pride reflected in the grounds of Pemberley, and are forced to admit that you have under-estimated Mr Darcy.

It wouldn't be the first time. Deduct 20 INTELLIGENCE POINTS.

On applying to see the house, you are admitted into the hall where you are met by the housekeeper. She is a respectable-looking elderly woman, and again, is much less fine, and more civil, than you had expected. You follow her through the door to the dining parlour and find a large, well-proportioned room, handsomely fitted up. You go to a window to enjoy its prospect: every disposition of the ground is good; and you look on the whole scene – the river, the trees scattered on its banks, and the winding of the valley, as far as you can trace it – with delight.

'And of this place,' you think, 'I might have been mistress!'

 Having second thoughts?

'Instead of viewing these rooms as a stranger, I might have rejoiced in them as my own, and welcomed to them as visitors my uncle and aunt. But no' – you recollect yourself, remembering Darcy's scruples concerning the 'inferiority of your connections' – 'that could never be: my uncle and aunt would have been lost to me; I should not have been allowed to invite them.'

This is a lucky recollection – it saves you from something like regret.

 Indeed. Collect 10 INTELLIGENCE POINTS.

You learn from Mrs Reynolds that Mr Darcy is expected tomorrow with a large party of friends and you rejoice that your own journey was not by any circumstance delayed a day. You pass through other rooms and Mrs Reynolds draws your attention to a likeness of Mr Darcy suspended amongst several other miniatures, over a mantelpiece.

'It is a handsome face,' says Mrs Gardiner, looking at the picture; 'but, Lizzy, you can tell us whether it is like or not.'

Mrs Reynolds's respect for you seems to increase on this intimation of your knowing her master.

 Which in turn increases your CONFIDENCE. Collect 10 points.

'Does that young lady know Mr Darcy?' she asks.

You colour, and say, 'A little.'

'And do not you think him a very handsome gentleman, ma'am?'

'Yes, very handsome,' you reply.

 Really? Since when have you been of this opinion? Since seeing his 'handsome' property by any chance?

'And he is such a good master,' she continues. 'I have never had a cross word from him in my life, and I have known him ever since he was four years old.'

That he is not a good-tempered man has been your firmest opinion and you are extremely surprised to hear her say otherwise. She goes on to say that it is no surprise to her that he has grown up so good-natured, since he was the 'sweetest-tempered, most generous-hearted boy in the world'.

You almost stare at her. 'Can this be Mr Darcy!' you think. You listen, wonder, doubt, and are impatient for more.

'He is the best landlord, and the best master,' she continues, 'that ever lived; not like the wild young men nowadays, who think of nothing but themselves.'

With a pang, you remember Mr Wickham.

'Some people call him proud;' she continues, 'but I am sure I never saw anything of it. To my fancy, it is only because he does not rattle away like other young men.'

You can hardly believe what you are hearing.

 Deduct 10 INTELLIGENCE POINTS for once again having underestimated Mr Darcy.

'In what an amiable light does this place him!' you think, amazed and astonished by Mrs Reynolds's account. Everything you have heard is contrary to what you had expected; everything is contrary to your own opinions of him.

'This fine account of him,' whispers your aunt as you walk on, 'is not quite consistent with his behaviour to our poor friend, Mr Wickham.'

'Perhaps we might be deceived,' you caution her.

'That is not very likely; our authority was too good.'

You earnestly wish to put her right, but judge that now is not the time.

 At last, a sound judgement.

On reaching the spacious lobby above, you are shown into the picture gallery. There are many family portraits, and you walk on in quest of the only face whose features are known to you. At last it arrests you – and you behold a striking resemblance to Mr Darcy, with such a smile over the face as you remember to have sometimes seen when he looked at you.

 Just thinking about it increases your CONFIDENCE. *Collect 10 points.*

You stand several minutes before the picture in earnest contemplation. At this moment, in your mind, there is a more gentle sensation towards the original than you have ever felt in the height of your acquaintance. What praise is more valuable than the praise of an intelligent servant? As a brother, a landlord, a master, you consider how many people's happiness are in his guardianship! As you stand before the canvas, you think of the regard he has shown you with a deeper sentiment of gratitude than ever before.

 It's a miracle it's taken you this long.

When all of the house that is open to general inspection has been seen, you return downstairs, and taking leave of the housekeeper, are consigned over to the gardener. He asks you which part of the grounds you would like to see first.

To go to the river first, turn to page 261.

To take the path across the park to the handsome woodland first, turn to page 268.

You refuse Mr Bennet as politely as you can and he leaves the house in an angry disgust. You quickly hurry to change your attire and do your best to catch up with your uncle and aunt at the concert. You make it to the Octagon Room just in time for the concert, and just in time to see Captain Wentworth entering the room accompanied by a woman with whom he is talking in a most intimate fashion. She is less beautiful than you are, and certainly older, and yet it seems there is something between them. You are overwhelmed with emotion when you see them, and for a moment you fear that you might faint.

 Deduct 50 CONFIDENCE POINTS.

Your aunt catches sight of you and rushes to your aid, expressing great surprise at seeing you there at all given that you refused the invitation. You endeavour to recover yourself and assure her that you are well, and that you are simply a little too hot after rushing to make it in time. You take your seat with your aunt and uncle and do your best to enjoy the concert but in truth your attention is wholly absorbed in watching Captain Wentworth and the remarkably plain lady.

 Deduct another 50 CONFIDENCE POINTS.

You are grateful that he has not seen you and during the interval you make your excuses to your aunt and uncle, and retire home early blaming a bad headache for your early departure. You really do have a bad headache in fact, and your spirits are quite depressed.

The following day you learn that Captain Wentworth is engaged to be married to the very lady with whom you saw him last night. It seems that the real reason he was so little affected by Louisa's engagement to Benwick is that he had likewise found love elsewhere while staying at Lyme during Louisa's convalescence. The lady is Miss Anne Elliot of Kellynch Hall[34] and she and Captain Wentworth are to be married next month. His attentions to you at the coffee shop were nothing more than polite concern and a way of showing you his forgiveness for the past. You are quite devastated. You don't think that you can take much more of this rejection and heartache, and resolve at last to leave all the responsibility of saving the Bennet family from homelessness to your sister Jane whom, in any case, you are sure will be married before long provided Bingley is not persuaded off her again following Lydia's patched-up marriage to Wickham.

THE END

Your frustration is understandable, but nobody likes a quitter. You have failed to complete your mission.

c) Deprecate the connection in every light.

Congratulations! You ruin, perhaps for ever, the happiness of your sister who withers away the rest of her years getting older and uglier and never again being loved by anyone. Your skills of Persuasion are top-notch! Well done.

 Collect 500 FORTUNE POINTS and add 'Top-Notch Persuasive Skills' to your list of ACCOMPLISHMENTS.

Continue on page 296.

As you walk across the lawn towards the river, you turn back to look again; and to your very great surprise, the owner of it himself suddenly comes forward from the road which leads behind it to the stables.

 Good God! What awful timing. You curse your unlucky stars. This time they agree: they deserve to be cursed.

Your eyes instantly meet, and both of you blush. He absolutely starts, and for a moment seems immovable from surprise; but shortly recovering himself, advances towards your party, and speaks to you, if not in terms of perfect composure, at least of perfect civility.

Astonished and confused, you scarcely dare lift your eyes to his face, and know not what answer you return to his civil enquiries after your family. His manner is greatly improved from what it was when you last parted at Rosings and you are amazed at the alteration. Every sentence that he utters increases your embarrassment; and every idea of the impropriety of your being found here recurs to your mind.

 It really does look as if you are throwing yourself in his way again. Deduct 20 FORTUNE POINTS.

The few minutes in which you continue together are some of the most uncomfortable of your life. Nor does he seem much more at ease: when he speaks, his accent has none of its usual sedateness; and he repeats his enquiries as to the time of your having left Longbourn, and of your stay in Derbyshire, so often, and in so hurried a way, as plainly speaks the distraction of his thoughts. At length every idea seems to fail him; and, after standing a few moments without saying a word, he suddenly recollects himself, and takes leave.

 Oh dear. Not a good sign. Deduct 20 CONFIDENCE POINTS.

The others then join you, and, wholly engrossed by your own feelings, you follow them in silence. You are overpowered by shame and vexation. How strange must your being there appear to him! You blush again and again over the perverseness of the meeting. And his behaviour, so strikingly altered – what can it mean? That he should even speak to you is amazing!

 True enough.

But to speak with such civility, to enquire after your family! Never in your life have you seen his manners so easy, never has he spoken with such gentleness as on this unexpected meeting. What a contrast it offers to his last address in Rosings Park, when he put his letter into your hand! You know not what to think, nor how to account for it.

You long to know in what manner he thinks of you. Whether he feels more of pain or of pleasure in seeing you, you cannot tell, but his parting suggests that he certainly does not see you with composure.

At length, the remarks of your companions on your absence of mind rouse you, and you feel the necessity of appearing more like yourself.

After walking for some time, you are making your way back towards the house on the opposite side of the river when you are again surprised by the sight of Mr Darcy approaching you, and at no great distance. You resolve to appear and to speak with calmness but in truth, your nerves are greatly discomposed.

With a glance you see that he has lost none of his recent civility; and, to imitate his politeness, you begin as you meet to admire the beauty of the place; but you have not got beyond the words 'delightful' and 'charming' when some unlucky recollections obtrude and you fancy that praise of Pemberley might make it seem as if you are, after all, hoping to become mistress of it!

 Whoops. Deduct 20 FORTUNE POINTS.

Your colour changes, and you say no more.

He asks if you will do him the honour of introducing him to your friends. You can hardly suppress a smile at his being now seeking the acquaintance of some of those very relations against whom his pride had revolted in his offer to you.

The introduction, however, is immediately made; and as you name their relationship to yourself, you steal a sly look at him, to see how he bears it. That he is *surprised* by the connection is evident from his expression; he sustains it, however, with fortitude, and, so far from decamping as fast as he can from such disgraceful companions, turns back with you, and enters into conversation with Mr Gardiner. You listen most attentively to all that passes between them, and glory in every expression, every sentence of your uncle's which marks his intelligence, his taste and his good manners.

 Thank God you have at least two SUPERIOR CONNECTIONS. *Add 'The Gardiners' to your list.*

The conversation soon turns upon fishing; and you hear Mr Darcy invite him to fish there as often as he chooses while he continues in the neighbourhood, offering at the same time to supply him with fishing tackle, and pointing out those parts of the stream where there is usually most sport. Your astonishment at his generosity is extreme.

But you are pleased. Collect 20 CONFIDENCE POINTS.

Continually you repeat to yourself, 'Why is he so altered? From what can it proceed? It cannot be for *me* – it cannot be for *my* sake that his manners are thus softened.' And yet you hope most earnestly that it is.

After walking some time in this way Mrs Gardiner goes to take her husband's arm and Mr Darcy takes her place by you as you walk. After a short silence, you speak. You wish him to know that you had been assured of his absence before you came to the place. He acknowledges that he was unexpected, and says that business with his steward had occasioned his coming forward a few hours before the rest of the party with whom he was travelling. 'They will join me early tomorrow,' he continues, 'and among them are some who will claim an acquaintance with you – Mr Bingley and his sisters.'

You remember the last time Mr Bingley was spoken of between you, and the colour rises in your cheeks.

Deduct 10 CONFIDENCE POINTS.

'But there is also one other person in the party who more particularly wishes to be known to you,' continues Mr Darcy. 'Will you allow me, or do I ask too much, to introduce my sister to your acquaintance during your stay at Lambton?'

The surprise of such an application is great indeed; it is too great for you to know in what manner you consent to it. You feel sincerely honoured.

 Collect 20 FORTUNE POINTS and 20 CONFIDENCE POINTS.

You now walk on in silence, each of you deep in thought. You are so surprised, so pleased by his change in manner and cannot help but wonder what he means by it. You want to believe that it is all for your benefit, that his feelings for you have not been entirely extinguished, but you chastise yourself for having such foolish hopes and thoughts. When you reach the carriage you are all pressed to go into the house and take some refreshment; but this is declined, and you part on each side with the utmost politeness. Mr Darcy hands you and your aunt into the carriage; and when it drives off, you see him walk slowly towards the house.

The observations of your uncle and aunt begin; and each pronounces Darcy to be infinitely superior to anything they had expected.

There's nothing for it now – you are forced to add 'Mr Darcy' to your list of SUPERIOR CONNECTIONS. Doing so instantly wins you 50 FORTUNE POINTS. Who'd have thought it?

Mrs Gardiner cannot reconcile Wickham's account of Darcy and his cruelty, with what she has seen of the man himself. Now that you are alone, you give them to understand, in as guarded a manner as you can without actually naming your authority, the nature of what you learnt from Mr Darcy, omitting the details concerning his sister. Mrs Gardiner is surprised and concerned; and when she has come to accept it, she regrets ever having seen Darcy in a bad light.

Your aunt's approval is invaluable. Collect 20 FORTUNE POINTS. It's about time she approved of someone you liked.

The rest of the day is spent with Mrs Gardiner's former acquaintances, but you have little attention for any of these new friends: you can do nothing but think, and think with wonder, of Mr Darcy's civility, and above all, of his wishing you to be acquainted with his sister. Whatever desire Miss Darcy might have of being acquainted with you must be the work of her brother, and, without looking further, it is satisfactory; it is gratifying to know that his resentment has not made him think really ill of you.

It really is a miracle.

The very next day Mr Darcy brings his sister to visit you and the formidable introduction takes place.

First impressions[35] are extremely important. You are keen
to make a good first impression on Miss Darcy, but are
unsure what she makes of you. She is outwardly polite, but
take the following **First Impressions Test** to find out
what Miss Darcy REALLY thinks of you!

*Mr Darcy has just made the formal introduction and it is now
your turn to speak.*

Do you

a) *Ask her how her journey was and then keep extremely quiet in
the hope that she won't realize how unsophisticated,
uneducated, unaccomplished, and unconnected you are.*

b) *Ask her how her journey was, make a few polite enquiries
about her health, comment on the weather but mostly keep
quiet to give her a chance to speak.*

c) *Ask her how her journey was; tell her how excessively you hate
long journeys yourself; how tiring your own journey to
Derbyshire was; how delighted you are with Derbyshire; how
shocked you were to hear about her and Mr Wickham; that you
never liked him yourself; assure her that she is better off without
him; offer to set her up with another, much more handsome
officer; tell her that you had heard she was excessively proud,
but that to you she only seems extremely shy; declare her your
new best friend; tell her how much you admire Pemberley and
ask her how much the chimneypiece cost.*

If you answered a), turn to page 331.

If you answered b), turn to page 317.

If you answered c), turn to page 295.

The gardener takes you across the park to the handsome woodlands, along a path that winds along the perimeter, and then along the river-bank back up to the house. You see and admire it all with great pleasure, and the gardener is able to tell you the history of the estate which your aunt and uncle find of great interest. You cannot quite give him your full attention, however, as your mind is somewhat distracted by memories of another history, told to you by both Darcy and Wickham.

When you have finished your tour you thank the gardener for his time, return to the carriage and take your leave of Pemberley, conscious of the fact that Darcy himself arrives tomorrow and once again thankful that your journey was not by any circumstance delayed a day.

You turn out of the park and on to the road to Lambton. Your companions talk little, tired from their walk, and you are therefore at liberty to indulge the melancholy reflections that the day has given rise to.

 Deduct 100 INTELLIGENCE POINTS for REPEATEDLY, and against all advice, going out of your way to make yourself more miserable than you already are.

It is hard not to think of Darcy arriving, hard not to think that he will be within five miles of you as of tomorrow, and hard not to wish that you could see him again and make him understand the very great change which your feelings have undergone since you last saw him. You wish him to understand how earnestly you regret blaming him for ruining Wickham's happiness, and to show him that, since reading his letter, you now have a fuller understanding of the situation and you no longer bear him any ill will for his part in harming Jane's.

But you can't. It's too late. Deduct 50 FORTUNE POINTS.

As your thoughts turn to Jane you are once more reminded that she has not written to you for a number of days and you are just beginning to wonder with concern why that could be when you hear the driver call 'Look out!' and at that moment you are run off the road by another carriage. You are thrown from your seat as your vehicle overturns and lands, upside down, crumpled by its own weight, in the ditch by the side of the road. With great difficulty, and suffering from the shock and a number of broken bones, do you manage to crawl from the wreckage, making your way through the broken carriage window, in great and overwhelming pain. When you have to some degree recovered your senses, your first thought is for your aunt and uncle. You call their names but there is no answer and you fear that they are trapped within the wreckage. You call for help, hoping that someone from the other carriage will come to your aid, and to your great joy and relief, you hear the sound of footsteps approaching. You turn your head to see what knight in shining armour is coming your way and to your great and all-encompassing horror, see only Miss Bingley.

'Good afternoon, Miss Bennet,' says she, looming over you with a smile of sneering and wholly inappropriate civility.

Terror grips you.

'I had heard that you were in the area. I was forced to rest and wait in a most squalid little inn at Lambton while my driver made a small repair to the carriage. Imagine my surprise when I happened to overhear one of the servants mentioning that Mr and Mrs Gardiner and their niece Miss Bennet were out for the day visiting *Pemberley*!'

You try to move but she stops you with a well-placed foot on your chest.

'Mr Darcy has been speaking of you a great deal too much lately, Miss Bennet. I won't stand for it. Who knows what witchcraft you have employed to catch his attention? Though you have made an impression of sorts, do you think a man such as Mr Darcy could ever seriously consider someone like you? Do you think he could ever be induced to marry a woman without family, connections, fortune, beauty or taste?'

You open your mouth to reply, but before you have a chance she screams at you, 'Not if I have anything to do with it!' And with that she returns to her carriage. You use all your strength to try and crawl out of the road, but your injuries are great and it is more than you can manage. Miss Bingley comes at you with great speed, runs over your already broken body, and hurtles off in the direction of Pemberley, leaving you for dead. Her methods are effective, and with a broken back and many internal injuries, it is not long before your consciousness slips away from you and into the welcoming arms of death.

THE END

It's safe to say you've failed to complete your mission.

You are interrupted by Mr Bingley who has likewise come to wait on you. Upon seeing him, your thoughts naturally fly to your sister and you quickly perceive that his do too when he observes to you, in a tone which has something of real regret, that it 'is a very long time since he had the pleasure of seeing Jane'; adding quickly, 'it is above eight months. We have not met since the 26th of November, when we were all dancing together at Netherfield.'

It is clear to you that Miss Darcy isn't a rival for Jane.

You were right, for once. Collect 10 INTELLIGENCE POINTS.

It is not often that you can turn your eyes on Mr Darcy himself; but, whenever you do you are pleased by what you see. Never, even in the company of his dear friends at Netherfield, or his dignified relations at Rosings, have you seen him so desirous to please, as now, when no importance can result from the success of his endeavours.

When they arise to depart, your visitors invite you to dinner. Mrs Gardiner looks at you, but you have turned away your head in momentary embarrassment. She ventures to engage for your attendance, and the day after the next is fixed on.

Eager to be alone, and fearful of enquiries or hints from your uncle and aunt, you stay with them only long enough to hear their favourable opinion of Bingley, and then hurry away to dress.

Your aunt suggests that you must return the politeness of Miss Darcy's early visit by calling on her the following morning. You are pleased; though when you ask yourself the reason, you have very little to say in reply.

 So much for your Self-Awareness.

You set off soon after breakfast, and on reaching the house are shown through the hall into a saloon where you are received most civilly by Miss Darcy. By Mrs Hurst and Miss Bingley you are noticed only by a curtsy, but even they cannot dampen your high spirits.

 Collect 10 CONFIDENCE POINTS.

Tea and cake is served, and not long afterwards Mr Darcy enters the room. No sooner does he appear than you wisely resolve to be perfectly easy and unembarrassed – a resolution the more necessary to be made because you see that the suspicions of the whole party are awakened against you both. Miss Darcy, on her brother's entrance, exerts herself much more to talk; and you see that he is anxious for you and his sister to get acquainted, and forwards as much as possible every attempt at conversation on either side. Miss Bingley sees all this likewise; and, with seeming jealousy, takes the first opportunity of saying, with sneering civility, 'Pray, Miss Eliza, are not the Hertfordshire militia removed from Meryton? They must be a great loss to *your* family.'

 Here we go again.

You instantly comprehend that she means Wickham and the various recollections connected with him give you a moment's distress; but exerting yourself vigorously to repel the ill-natured attack, you confirm that the militia have indeed left Meryton, answering the question in a tolerably disengaged tone.

 Collect 50 bonus FORTUNE POINTS.

Darcy, with a heightened complexion, earnestly looks at you, and his sister, her thoughts evidently flying to her attempted elopement with Wickham, is overcome with confusion and unable to lift up her eyes. Even Miss Bingley, if she knew what pain she was then giving her beloved friend, would undoubtedly have refrained from the hint.

Your visit does not continue long after this question and answer, and Mr Darcy attends you to your carriage. You return to Lambton with your head full of him.

--------≫●≪--------

Desiring news from your sister, you were a good deal disappointed in not finding a letter from Jane on your first arrival at Lambton; and this disappointment has been renewed on each of the mornings since; but on the third morning you receive two letters at once, the first one marked as having been mis-sent elsewhere.

You had just been preparing to walk as the letters came in; and your uncle and aunt, leaving you to enjoy them in quiet, set off by themselves. The one mis-sent must be first attended to; it was written five days ago. Nothing could have prepared you for what you now read: your fifteen-year-old sister Lydia has eloped with Wickham.

 It's the worst possible news. Deduct 50 FORTUNE POINTS.

Worse still, there is reason to fear she and Wickham are not gone to Gretna Green to be married.

 It's even worse than the worst possible news. Deduct another 50 FORTUNE POINTS.

Lydia's short letter to Mrs Forster, with whom she was staying in Brighton, gave them to understand that they were going to Gretna Green, but something was dropped by Wickham's friend and your acquaintance, the officer Denny, expressing his belief that Wickham never intended to go there, or to marry Lydia at all.

 Just when you thought things couldn't get any worse, they do. Deduct 100 FORTUNE POINTS.

Colonel Forster, taking the alarm, set off from Brighton, intending to follow their route but could trace them no further than Clapham. Jane begs you all to go to Longbourn as soon as possible; your father is going to London with Colonel Forster instantly but your uncle's advice and assistance is longed for.

 Your life is utterly ruined. The shame of such a family scandal will not be easily recovered from, and all hopes of ever reigniting Mr Darcy's affections must now be entirely cast aside. You lose 200 CONFIDENCE POINTS, 200 FORTUNE POINTS and all hope of future happiness, in one fell swoop.

'Oh! Where, where is my uncle?' you cry, darting from your seat, but as you reach the door it is opened by a servant, and Mr Darcy appears. Your pale face and impetuous manner make him start, and before he can recover himself enough to speak, you hastily exclaim, 'I beg your pardon, but I must leave you. I must find Mr Gardiner this moment, on business that cannot be delayed; I have not an instant to lose.'

'Good God! What is the matter?' he cries, with more feeling than politeness; then recollecting himself, 'I will not detain you a minute; but let me, or the servant, go after Mr and Mrs Gardiner. You are not well enough; you cannot go yourself.'

His kindness only makes it worse. You hesitate, but your knees tremble under you, and you feel how little would be gained by your attempting to pursue the Gardiners. Calling back the servant, therefore, you commission him, though in so breathless an accent as makes you almost unintelligible, to fetch his master and mistress home instantly.

On his quitting the room you sit down, unable to support yourself, and looking so miserably ill that Darcy says, in a tone of gentleness and commiseration, 'Let me call your maid. Is there nothing you could take to give you present relief? A glass of wine – shall I get you one? You are very ill.'

'No, I thank you,' you reply, endeavouring to recover yourself. 'There is nothing the matter with me. I am quite well.'

It is clear, however, that something is dreadfully wrong, and you are on the point of telling him the truth when you suddenly recollect yourself.

 Just in time. Collect 10 INTELLIGENCE POINTS.

The situation is critical. If you tell Darcy what has happened, then all chance of any form of friendship with him must be entirely lost. If you do not tell him, there is a chance that the situation between Lydia and Wickham might perhaps be resolved. Though Darcy could never marry into a family that counted Mr Wickham among its sons, it is perhaps still possible that you could maintain an acquaintance. You need to make a decision. Fast.

To tell Mr Darcy the truth, turn to page 279.

To conceal the truth from him and attempt to save some semblance of friendship, however trifling, turn to page 291.

You politely decline their invitation, and settle in for an evening of reading and reflection. The Philipses have not been gone long when you hear a knock at the door, and the housemaid's voice soon announcing the name of Mr Bennet. He appears surprised to find you alone, and begs your forgiveness for the intrusion. Though you had hoped to spend the evening alone, you assure him that his presence is not unwelcome and offer him a seat. After talking for some time on trivial matters, Mr Bennet suddenly gets up and comes to sit next to you on the sofa. He takes your hand in his, and to your great surprise begins to pay his addresses to you.

'I knew you by report long before you came to Bath,' says he, with meaning. 'I have heard about your person, your disposition, your accomplishments and your manner. I have many years ago received such a description of Elizabeth Bennet as has inspired me with the highest idea of your merit, and excited the warmest curiosity to know you.'

You cannot disguise your surprise.

'The name of Elizabeth Bennet has long had an interesting sound to me,' he goes on. 'Very long has it possessed a charm over my fancy; and now that we are alone, allow me to dare to share my wishes that the name might never change.'

You blush at such a description of yourself, and are overcome with surprise as you realize that Mr Bennet is actually proposing to you. You know not what to think. Until Captain Wentworth's return you had received Mr Bennet's attentions with pleasure, nay had actually encouraged them. But since seeing Captain Wentworth again, and learning that he is not to be married to Louisa after all, you find that you do not feel for Mr Bennet quite what you thought you did. What's more, try as you might, you still haven't learnt to forget Mr Darcy.

A difficult choice now lies before you. Mr Bennet is handsome indeed, but it seems now that there is a chance that things might work out with Captain Wentworth after all, and you still haven't quite succeeded in banishing all thoughts of Mr Darcy. There is an added incentive for marrying Mr Bennet which you have not fully considered before now: had he not been disowned by his father, Mr Bennet – and not Mr Collins – would have been next in line for the entail of the Longbourn estate. Marrying him would signal an official reintroduction into the family, and your sisters and mother would all be saved from the possibility of being thrown out of their home by Mr and Mrs Collins.

To accept Mr Bennet, turn to page 330.

To reject him and keep trying with Captain Wentworth,
turn to page 258. If you run, you might make it to
the concert before it starts.

'No, I am not ill,' you repeat. 'I am only distressed by some dreadful news I have just received from Longbourn.'

 That's an understatement.

You burst into tears as you allude to it, and for a few minutes cannot speak another word. At length you speak again. 'I have just had a letter from Jane, with such dreadful news. It cannot be concealed from anyone. My youngest sister has left all her friends – has eloped; has thrown herself into the power of... of Mr Wickham. They are gone off together from Brighton. *You* know him too well to doubt the rest. She has no money, no connections, nothing that can tempt him to... She is lost forever.'

Darcy is fixed in astonishment. You earnestly regret him knowing.

 Deduct 50 FORTUNE POINTS.

'But is it certain – absolutely certain?' he asks.

'Oh yes! They left Brighton together on Sunday night, and were traced almost to London, but not beyond: they are certainly not gone to Gretna Green.'

'And what has been done, what has been attempted, to recover her?'

'My father is gone to London, and Jane has written to beg my uncle's immediate assistance; and we shall be off, I hope, in half an hour. But nothing can be done – I know very well that nothing can be done. How is such a man to be worked on? How are they even to be discovered? I have not the smallest hope. It is every way horrible!'

 It's true. Deduct another 100 FORTUNE POINTS.

Darcy seems scarcely to hear you, and is walking up and down the room in earnest meditation, his brow contracted, his air gloomy. You soon observe, and instantly understand it. Your power is sinking; everything *must* sink under such a proof of family weakness, such an assurance of the deepest disgrace.

 Deduct 100 FORTUNE POINTS and 100 CONFIDENCE POINTS.

At this moment you understand your own wishes for the first time; and never have you so honestly felt that you could have loved him, as now, when all love must be in vain.

 If you have any FORTUNE POINTS left, you lose them all now.

Mr Darcy fears you have long been desiring his absence and wishes there were something he could do or say to offer consolation to such distress. He again expresses his sorrow for your distress, wishes it a happier conclusion than there is at present reason to hope, and after leaving his compliments for your relations, with only one serious, parting look, goes away.

Mr and Mrs Gardiner hurry back in alarm, and after the first exclamations of surprise and horror, Mr Gardiner readily promises every assistance in his power. You set off for Longbourn as soon as possible and, sleeping one night on the road, reach Longbourn by dinner-time the next day. There is little to learn from Jane: your father is in town but will not write till he has something of importance to mention; your mother refuses to leave her dressing room. Jane shows you Lydia's letter, which is thoughtless and vain but does at least show that *she* believed they were going to Gretna Green to be married. Not that it makes much difference now.

Your whole party is in hopes of a letter from Mr Bennet the next morning, but the post comes in without bringing a single line from him. Mr Gardiner waits only for the letters before he sets off for London. Every day at Longbourn is now a day of anxiety; but the most anxious part of each is when the post is expected. Through letters, whatever of good or bad is to be told will be communicated, and every succeeding day is expected to bring some news of importance.

Mr Gardiner writes with information he has learnt from corresponding with Colonel Forster, but it is not good. It transpires that Wickham left gaming debts behind him to a very considerable amount.

 Oh dear.

Colonel Forster believes that more than a thousand pounds will be necessary to clear his expenses at Brighton. He owes a good deal to the merchants and tavern keepers in the town, but his debts of honour to his friends there are still more formidable.

 Can things get any worse?

Rendered spiritless by the ill-success of all their endeavours, Mr Bennet yields to his brother-in-law's entreaty that he would return to his family, and leaves it to him to continue their pursuit. Two days after Mr Bennet's return an express comes for him from Mr Gardiner. He has seen them both; they are not married, nor can he find there was any intention of being so; but if Mr Bennet is willing to assure to Lydia, by settlement, her equal share of the five thousand pounds secured among you all after his death and enter into an engagement of allowing her, during his life, one hundred pounds per annum, they will very soon be married.

'They must marry,' says Mr Bennet. 'There is nothing else to be done. But there are two things that I want very much to know: one is, how much money your uncle has laid down, to bring it about; and the other, how I am ever to pay him. No man in his senses would marry Lydia on so slight a temptation as one hundred a year during my life, and fifty after I am gone. Wickham's a fool if he takes her with a farthing less than ten thousand pounds.'

Apparently, they can.

Your shock is great indeed; you wanted to hear that they were married, but never in your wildest dreams had you imagined what a price would have to be paid to achieve it.

Deduct 20 INTELLIGENCE POINTS for your naivety.

Shame for your sister's actions once again overcomes you. Mrs Bennet can hardly contain herself for joy, and in vain do you remind her what an obligation your uncle's actions have put you all under.

You are now most heartily sorry that from the distress of the moment, you were led to make Mr Darcy acquainted with your fears for your sister; for since her marriage will so shortly give the proper termination to the elopement, you might hope to conceal its unfavourable beginning from all those who were not immediately on the spot.

Deduct 20 INTELLIGENCE POINTS for having told him.

It is not to be supposed that Mr Darcy will connect himself with a family where, to every other objection, will now be added an alliance and relationship of the nearest kind with the man whom he so justly scorns. You are humbled, you are grieved; you repent, though you hardly know of what. You are convinced that you could be happy with him, when it is no longer likely you should meet.

Deduct 50 CONFIDENCE POINTS.

You begin now to comprehend that he is exactly the man who, in disposition and talents, would most suit you. It was a union that would be to the advantage of both; by your ease and liveliness, his mind might be softened, his manners improved; and from his judgement, information, and knowledge of the world, you must receive benefit of greater importance. But no such happy marriage can now teach the admiring multitude what connubial felicity really is.

You have no FORTUNE POINTS left to lose. If you have any CONFIDENCE POINTS left, deduct all of those instead.

Mr Gardiner soon writes again to say that Mr Wickham has resolved on quitting the mobile military force of the militia in favour of the fixed-camp regular army. He has the promise of an ensigncy in General —'s regiment, now quartered in the north. You feel all the advantages of Wickham's removal from the area but Mrs Bennet is not so well pleased with the distance that is to be put between her and Lydia.

The wedding day arrives. The carriage is sent to meet the newlyweds, and they are at Longbourn by dinner-time. Their arrival is greeted with rapture by your mother who throws her arms around Lydia and fawns over her new son-in-law.

You are disgusted by Lydia's behaviour as she turns from sister to sister, demanding your congratulations. Wickham is scarcely better, and shows no sense of the shame of his situation, or the trouble and anxiety he has caused you all. They each of them seem to have the happiest memories in the world. You urge Lydia to act more modestly, endeavouring to make her sensible of the pain she has caused, but nothing you say has any influence whatsoever.

Your Lack of Influence is once more forcibly impressed upon you. Deduct 10 INTELLIGENCE POINTS.

Lydia and Wickham are not to remain above ten days with you and no one but your mother regrets that their stay is so short.

One morning, soon after their arrival, as she is sitting with you and Jane, Lydia gives you an account of every moment leading up to her wedding. You think that there cannot be too little said on the subject but she insists on giving you every detail. It is as she does so that she lets slip that Mr Darcy was present and had attended Mr Wickham. You are utterly amazed.

'But gracious me!' exclaims Lydia, 'I quite forgot! I ought not to have said a word about it. I promised them so faithfully! What will Wickham say? It was to be such a secret!'

'If it was to be secret,' says Jane, 'say not another word on the subject. You may depend upon my seeking no further.'

Just for this moment, you wish Jane was not always so uncompromisingly virtuous.

'Oh! Certainly,' you add, though burning with curiosity, 'we will ask you no questions.'

Conjectures as to the meaning of Mr Darcy's being at your sister's wedding, rapid and wild, hurry into your brain; but you are satisfied with none. You cannot bear such suspense; and hastily seizing a sheet of paper, write a short letter to your aunt, to request an explanation of the intelligence Lydia dropped.

You receive an answer very quickly. She is greatly surprised that you do not already know the details. Not long after your uncle had arrived in London to help in the search for your sister he received a visit from Mr Darcy who had found out where Lydia and Wickham were. He had left Derbyshire the day after you did to find them out, blaming himself for not making Wickham's true character publicly known.

 Collect 20 bonus FORTUNE POINTS.

He had called it, therefore, his duty to step forward, and endeavour to remedy an evil which had been brought on by himself. He discovered them through a Mrs Younge, who was some time ago governess to Miss Darcy, and was dismissed from her charge following Miss Darcy's own scrape with Wickham. He tried to persuade Lydia to quit her present disgraceful situation, and return to her friends as soon as they could be prevailed on to receive her, offering his assistance as far as it would go. But Lydia was determined to be married and cared not when. Since such were her feelings, it only remained, he thought, to secure and expedite a marriage which, in his very first conversation with Wickham, he easily learnt had never been *his* design. They met several times, for there was much to be discussed. Wickham, of course, wanted more than he could get, but at length was induced to be reasonable.

Nothing was to be done that Mr Darcy did not do himself. Your uncle and Mr Darcy battled it together for a long time, but at last your uncle was forced to yield.

 It is almost incredible. Collect 200 FORTUNE POINTS.

Instead of being allowed to be of use to his niece, Mr Gardiner was forced to put up with only being given the credit for it.

The contents of this letter throw you into a flutter of spirits. Your heart whispers that he did it for you, but it is a hope shortly checked by other considerations, and you soon feel that even your vanity is insufficient, when required to depend on his affection for you, for a woman who had already refused him, as able to overcome a sentiment so natural as abhorrence against relationship with Wickham. Brother-in-law of Wickham! Every kind of pride must revolt from the connection.

 You'll be lucky to attract any *man after this most recent scandal, never mind a man like Mr Darcy. Deduct 20 INTELLIGENCE POINTS.*

It is painful, exceedingly painful, to know that you are under obligations to a person who can never receive a return. Oh! How heartily do you grieve over every ungracious sensation you ever encouraged, every saucy speech you ever directed towards him. For yourself, you are humbled; but you are proud of him.

Proud that in a cause of compassion and honour he was able to get the better of himself.

 You have finally come to a true understanding of the concept of Pride. Took your time, didn't you?

 Add 'True Understanding of Pride' to your list of ACCOMPLISH-MENTS, and collect 200 FORTUNE POINTS. You need all the money you can get the way things are going.

The day of Wickham and Lydia's departure soon comes, and your mother is forced to submit to a separation which is likely to continue at least a twelvemonth.

Peace once again returns to Longbourn, and you must now do your best to put Mr Darcy from your mind. A week after Lydia and Wickham's departure, you receive an invitation from the Philipses to join them on a trip to Bath.

If you feel you might benefit from a holiday after recent events, turn to page 313 to accept the invitation.

If you are tired of all these trips away, and would rather rest quietly at home and indulge in your favourite pastime of making yourself even more miserable than you already are, turn to page 328.

You refuse Captain Wentworth, to his great and evident distress. He can hardly believe that you have broken his heart again, in exactly the same way that you did three years ago. You can hardly believe it either, and hurry away as soon as you can.

Add 'Remorseless Heartbreaker' to your list of FAILINGS.

You return to Longbourn at the earliest opportunity and open your heart to Jane, whose concern and astonishment are equal at hearing all that has passed in Bath. When you retire to bed at night, you wonder what will become of you both, and whether Mr Bingley will ever come back for Jane. Since Lydia's marriage to Wickham, your hopes have diminished. No matter how much he might have loved Jane, and indeed might still love her, it seems unlikely to you that Bingley would ever willingly attach himself to a family with such a recent scandal marring its name.

Recalling the scandal naturally leads your thoughts once again to Mr Darcy, to whom your whole family will forever be in debt for his part in securing Lydia's marriage. You have heard nothing of him since and have done your best to put hopes of ever seeing him again, and the idea that he might have helped Lydia for your sake alone, far from your mind. If Bingley, who has nothing like Darcy's reasons, is unlikely to associate with you after the scandal, it is hardly possible that Darcy ever could. It is with difficulty that you at last put these troubling reflections to the back of your mind and fall asleep.

Congratulations! You have completed Stage Four.

It took you long enough.

Will this ever end?

Turn to page 333 to find out.

450 *OR ABOVE*

You are currently more intelligent than Captain Wentworth and this is likely to result in a very unhappy marriage. With brains like this you could do better than Captain Wentworth anyway; after all, at one time he thought Louisa Musgrove a suitable match. Fortunately you realize just in time. It wouldn't take him long to teach you how to tie a few impressive nautical knots, and then you'd have nothing else to learn from him.

 It's harsh, but true. Captain Wentworth is not the man for you, you'd only regret it if you married him.

Continue on page 288 and raise your standards.

You conceal the truth from him and at your own insistence he soon afterwards takes leave of you. Mr and Mrs Gardiner hurry back in alarm, and as you tell them the news, you burst into tears. After the first exclamations of surprise and horror, Mr Gardiner readily promises every assistance in his power. You set off for Longbourn as soon as possible and, sleeping one night on the road, reach Longbourn by dinner-time the next day. There is little to learn from Jane: your father is in town but will not write till he has something of importance to mention; your mother does not yet leave her dressing room.

Jane shows you Lydia's letter, which is thoughtless and vain but does at least show that *she* believed they were going to Gretna Green to be married.

Your whole party is in hopes of a letter from Mr Bennet the next morning, but the post comes in without bringing a single line from him.

Deduct 20 FORTUNE POINTS.

Mr Gardiner waits only for the letters before he sets off for London.

Three days pass without any news, and when it does come, it is the worst kind. Wickham and Lydia were discovered on the first day of Mr Gardiner's arrival in London, and both he and your father prevailed upon Wickham to marry Lydia. Wickham's demands were high, however, far too high for your father and uncle and they were unable, even between them, to settle upon Lydia sufficient funds. When they returned the following day, Wickham was gone. He has deserted your sister

Lydia, giving no indication as to where he has gone. Your father and uncle initially set about trying to find him, but soon gave up the cause as hopeless.

Lydia is brought home and it is soon discovered that she is with child. She is utterly ruined, and your family honour is entirely crushed by the disgrace of this most horrific scandal and nobody ever talks to you again. You would leave the neighbourhood, but are so miserably poor you cannot afford to. Your father dies of a heart attack shortly afterwards and Mr Collins remorselessly turns you out of your house and leaves you to find your way in the world. Thanks to Lydia, you cannot even get work as a governess and it is not long before you find yourself in a debtors' prison, where you end your days in solitude and sadness, regretting the past and all that you have lost.

THE END

Guess what? You failed.

BELOW 450

Your intelligence is suitably average for the ever-so-slightly average Captain Wentworth.

You accept his proposal and after your average wedding you remove to your husband's average estate and live off your average fortune. You are occasionally visited by your average connections and you otherwise spend your days practising your average accomplishments.

THE END

Does this sound like a happy marriage to you?

If not, just this once you can return to page 327 and choose again.

Otherwise, congratulations! You've completed your mission.

a) Let Kitty come to her own decision.

You're not even trying; your Persuasive skills are abysmal.

 No wonder your father didn't listen to you when you advised him not to let Lydia go to Brighton. Deduct 100 FORTUNE POINTS.

Continue on page 296.

You have made the worst first impression you have ever made in your life.

Miss Darcy hates you. Though she is outwardly warm and polite she joins Miss Bingley and Mrs Hurst in abusing you whenever she can, starts looking around for more eligible young women for her brother and influences him against you at every opportunity.

 Deduct 200 FORTUNE POINTS and 100 INTELLIGENCE POINTS.

Continue on page 271.

Seeing Captain Wentworth again so unexpectedly has thrown your mind into great turmoil. When you vowed to put Mr Darcy from your mind, little did you expect to be visited by this ghost from your past! As your feelings for Mr Darcy have grown over these past weeks, the memory of your attachment to Captain Wentworth has been always at the back of your mind.

Strumpet.

You had endeavoured to forget him, but only because you were certain you would never see each other again. Now however, you are thrown into a state of great confusion. Your feelings for Captain Wentworth were more than equal to those you have lately felt for Darcy, and a first attachment is perhaps always the strongest.

You feel the necessity of returning indoors, and when you do you are relieved to discover that Captain Wentworth has left. Your cousins tax you with a thousand eager and curious questions but you give little away. You give them to understand that you made his acquaintance some years before, and were merely a little surprised to see him again. You blame the heat of the room, and your fatigue from the previous day's long journey for your need to get a little air, and thankfully their attention is soon taken away by the arrival of some other acquaintances with whom Charles is eager to converse over the matter of a double-barrel gun. Fortunately for you, neither the Philipses nor the Musgroves know anything about your previous engagement to Captain Wentworth since it was never spoken of again by you or Mrs Gardiner. You earnestly hope that you can conceal it for the duration of your stay at Bath, and pray that you will not often be in the same company as Captain Wentworth.

Your prayers are not answered, however.

 It was worth a try.

From this time you and Captain Wentworth are repeatedly in the same circle owing to his friendship with your cousin Charles. You have no conversation together, however, and no intercourse but what the commonest civility requires. You know not what to think and long to know what he feels for you now. You are soon spared all suspense however when Mary reveals to you that Captain Wentworth said he considers you 'so altered he should not have known you again'.

 Ouch.

Though you smart when you hear it, you do not think it is true, and put it down to his lingering resentment towards you for the past. From his behaviour to you, and some further hints that he drops in the general conversation, it becomes clear that Captain Wentworth has not forgiven you. He ignores you as much as possible, and when he cannot, is unpleasant to you. From what you can gather, it is certain that he feels that you used him ill, deserted and disappointed him; and worse, showed a feebleness of character in doing so.

 Add 'Feebleness of Character' to your list of FAILINGS.

You cannot entirely blame him. You rejected him in the belief that you were acting in his best interests, but it would seem that

297

you sacrificed his happiness along with your own, and you cannot escape the thought that it might, perhaps, have been all for nothing.

 Oh dear, another grave error of judgement. Deduct 50 INTELLIGENCE POINTS.

His cold civility cuts you to the quick, and it is with great difficulty that you maintain your characteristic good humour in the situation. To add to your difficulties, it quickly becomes apparent that Louisa Musgrove greatly admires the captain, and worse still, that the admiration is reciprocated. They are always together, and always gay. You cannot help but be a little surprised that Wentworth should be attracted to a girl as frivolous and flighty as Louisa; her character is so different from your own. He was always wont to value good sense above all else, but time perhaps has changed his tastes.

You do your best to be civil and polite to Captain Wentworth, and avoid being in his company more often than necessary by spending more time with your uncle and aunt Philips.

Collect 10 INTELLIGENCE POINTS.

You cannot avoid him entirely, however, and since your cousins know nothing of your history, it is difficult to always find excuses not to see them when they are with the captain.

One morning, about this time, the Musgroves propose a walk in the countryside around Bath and you feel it would do you good to go. You have told yourself many times that Captain Wentworth is lost to you now, and you are determined to meet him with composure, and to witness his attentions to Louisa without regret or ill-will. This walk is an excellent opportunity to put your resolution to the test and so you agree to it readily.

You occupy your mind as much as possible by musing on the beauty of the countryside; but you cannot help trying to catch the conversation between Captain Wentworth and Louisa.

How rude of you. Add 'Eavesdropping' to your list of FAILINGS.

You just overhear Louisa criticizing her sister-in-law and your cousin Mary for always being so easily persuaded by all those around her, even on matters of great importance, and asserting that she would never allow herself to be so.

'When I have made up my mind, I have made it!' she exclaims in conclusion.

Your feelings for Louisa at this moment can be well imagined. Knowing what he thinks of you for having changed your mind at the instigation of another, you almost dread Captain Wentworth's response, but strain to hear it nonetheless.

Naughty, naughty.

'Too yielding and indecisive a character is the worst of all evils,' replies Captain Wentworth. 'Let those who would be happy be firm. My first wish for all whom I am concerned for, is that they should be firm.'

You catch his deeper meaning and feel it very keenly.

Serves you right for eavesdropping.

You know he is thinking and talking with you in mind, and though he does not know that you are listening, you almost feel as if he is talking directly to you.

'If Louisa Musgrove would be beautiful and happy in her November of life,' he continues, 'she will cherish all her present powers of mind.'

You feel immediately that you have failed in your resolution. To hear Captain Wentworth talk to Louisa as he once talked to you cuts you deeply and you can no longer deny your feelings of the most unreasonable jealousy!

 This is news only to you. Deduct 10 INTELLIGENCE POINTS for failing to own your jealousy sooner.

You do your best to shake off the immediate depression of your spirits by remembering that even if Captain Wentworth does not love you any more, you have received more than one other proposal since his, and have even managed to attract the great Mr Darcy of Pemberley once!

 You have broken your vow to forget Mr Darcy. Deduct 20 INTELLIGENCE POINTS.

As you are thinking of Mr Darcy you suddenly remember when he told you at Netherfield about the implacability of his resentments. It seems that Captain Wentworth and Mr Darcy have more than a little in common, and you laugh to yourself when you think that you should be attracted to not one, but two stubborn and unforgiving men! You wonder what it must say about your own character, and then consider how unfortunate it is for your own happiness given the circumstances surrounding your attachment to each of these men. Where you are most in need of forgiveness, you are least likely to receive it.

Add 'Failure to Learn from Past Mistakes' to your list of FAILINGS.

You all return home to your lodgings and making your excuses to your aunt and uncle, you retire to your room to reflect on the morning. Everything now marks out Louisa for Captain Wentworth. You cannot really be angry with either of them; you had your chance three years ago, and you let it go.

 Deduct 100 INTELLIGENCE POINTS.

You feel the danger of dwelling on these melancholy reflections for too long, and do your best to shake them off by once more joining your aunt and uncle downstairs.

A few days later, Captain Wentworth proposes a trip to the seaside town of Lyme, to visit an old friend by the name of Captain Harville. Everyone is wild to go, and will not think of going without you.

 Except Captain Wentworth, who would gladly leave you behind.

You have little choice; you must submit to the plan, though you foresee little pleasure in being forced to watch the unfolding romance between Louisa and Wentworth with no means of escape.

 Deduct 10 FORTUNE POINTS.

You all set off at the appointed time and arrive at Lyme earlier than expected. After securing accommodations, and ordering a dinner at the inn, you all walk directly down to the sea. Captain Wentworth calls on his friends the Harvilles, while you and the rest of the party walk on towards the famous harbour wall, the Cobb, where Wentworth will join you. He soon arrives with Captain and Mrs Harville, and a Captain Benwick, who is staying with them. Captain Harville is tall and fair; and his manner open and agreeable. His wife is plain but warm and unaffected. Their friend Captain Benwick is shorter than Captain Harville but is perhaps more handsome, and his dark features become him well.

You all meet, and are introduced. You learn that Captain Benwick had been engaged to Captain Harville's sister, Fanny, who died the preceding summer, while Benwick was at sea. In mourning for Fanny, he now lives entirely with the Harvilles. You feel for Captain Benwick's loss, and it is evident that he still suffers under it.

After a pleasant walk you and the Musgroves return to the inn to dress and dine. Captain Harville visits in the evening and brings Captain Benwick with him. Benwick is shy, and disposed to abstraction; but he soon warms to your ease and openness. He is evidently a young man of considerable taste in reading, and you discuss poetry with him as best you can, though in truth you have read little beyond Cowper. Over the course of the evening you grow to like Captain Benwick more and more, and he is a welcome distraction from Louisa and Captain Wentworth who continue to ignore you and flirt in your company most unpleasantly.

 Add 'Captain Benwick' to your list of SUPERIOR CONNECTIONS and collect 20 FORTUNE POINTS.

Before he leaves, Captain Harville thanks you for showing such kind attention to the afflicted Benwick, and you assure him that it was a pleasure. You are not just being polite by saying it either; you really have enjoyed Captain Benwick's company and hope to see him again tomorrow.

The next morning, before breakfast, you take a walk down to the sea with the rest of your party, and to your delight, chance upon Captain Benwick who is likewise taking advantage of the sea air. He greets you all with pleasure and joins your party, once again seeking you out in particular, and conversing with you on such an intimate footing that you can hardly believe that it is only the second time you have met with him. As you are ascending the steps back up from the beach you pass a gentleman who politely draws back to let you by. As you pass he looks at you with a degree of earnest admiration which you cannot be insensible of.

 Now there's a first. Collect 30 CONFIDENCE POINTS.

You are looking remarkably well, it is true; the sea air has done you a world of good. It is evident that the gentleman admires you exceedingly and Captain Wentworth looks round at you instantly in a way which suggests that he has seen the look the gentleman has given you, and that just for this moment, he too thinks you worthy of admiration.

Collect another 30 CONFIDENCE POINTS.

You cannot help wondering if he thinks you 'so altered he would not have known you' *now*.

You bid farewell to the handsome Captain Benwick and return to the inn in high spirits. You have nearly done breakfast, when the sound of a carriage draws half the party to the window. The owner of the curricle is the same man you met this morning, who is at this very moment taking leave of the inn. You learn from the waiter that his name is Mr Bennet, a gentleman of large fortune, on his way to Bath.

'Bennet! Bless me!' cries Mary, 'it must be our cousin; it must be our Mr Bennet, it must, indeed! How very extraordinary! In the very same inn with us! Lizzy, must not it be our Mr Bennet?'

Mr Bennet is from a branch of your family that your father did not get on well with, and a family quarrel cut off this Mr Bennet from your notice. You all wonder at the coincidence of meeting him here.

He's a good-looking gentleman with a handsome carriage, and is related to you. Add him to your list of SUPERIOR CONNECTIONS, and give yourself 50 bonus FORTUNE POINTS. Who cares if you know nothing about him? He thought you were admirable, and that's all that counts.

Soon after breakfast Captain Benwick joins you again, to take a walk about Lyme. He is once again most attentive to you, so much so that more than once do you catch Mary smiling expressively at you as the captain asks your opinions on books, art and even philosophy. When you can be sure the captain cannot see you, you throw Mary a reproachful look, anxious lest the sensitive Benwick should see her teasing smiles. In truth, however, you are flattered by the captain's attentions and do little to discourage them. After exploring the town, you walk to the Cobb but there is too much wind to make the high part pleasant, and you all agree to get down the steps to the lower. You are all content to pass quietly and carefully down the steep flight, excepting Louisa: she must be jumped down them by Captain Wentworth. You find her impulsiveness petulant, though Captain Wentworth seems to find it charming.

 You are ragingly jealous, but at least you're keeping it to yourself. Collect 10 INTELLIGENCE POINTS.

You wonder at him for indulging her in such a dangerous game, but it seems there is nothing he will not do to make her happy. She is safely down, and instantly to show her enjoyment, runs up the steps to be jumped down again. He advises her against it, thinks the jar too great; but she smiles and says, 'I am determined I will.' He puts out his hands; she is too precipitate by half a second, she falls on the pavement on the Lower Cobb, and is taken up lifeless!

 Whoops.

There is no wound, no blood, no visible bruise; but her eyes are closed, she breathes not, her face is like death. Captain Wentworth catches her up, kneels with her in his arms and looks on her with a face as pallid as her own, in an agony of silence.

'She is dead! She is dead!' screams Mary. She sinks under the conviction and loses her senses too. She would have fallen on the steps, but for you and Captain Benwick, who catch and support her between you.

'Is there no one to help me?' are the first words which burst from Captain Wentworth, in a tone of despair.

'Go to him, go to him,' you cry to Captain Benwick. 'I can support her myself. Rub her hands, rub her temples; here are salts: take them, take them.'

Add 'First-Aid Skills' to your list of ACCOMPLISHMENTS.

Captain Benwick obeys, and Louisa is raised up and supported more firmly between them and Charles. Everything is done that you prompted, but in vain. Captain Wentworth, staggering against the wall for his support, exclaims in the bitterest agony, 'Oh God! Her father and mother! How is the news to be broken?'

'A surgeon!' you cry. 'Captain Benwick, you must know where a surgeon is to be found?'

Captain Benwick resigns the poor corpse-like figure entirely to the brother's care, and sets off for the town with the utmost rapidity.

'Lizzy, Lizzy,' cries Charles, 'what is to be done next? What, in heaven's name, is to be done next?'

Captain Wentworth's eyes are also turned towards you.

 You can't help but be gratified, though you really ought to be concentrating on the matter in hand. Collect 10 CONFIDENCE POINTS.

You instruct them to carry her gently to the inn, and you are making your way thither when you are met at the end of the Cobb by Captain Harville who insists that Louisa is taken to his house to await the surgeon.

The surgeon is with you almost before it seems possible. You are all sick with worry while he examines her. He is by no means hopeless, however, and though her head received a severe contusion, he has seen greater injuries recovered from.

The tone, the look, with which 'Thank God!' is uttered by Captain Wentworth, is something you are sure you will never forget. His love for Louisa is clear.

*For a moment you wish she **had** died. Add 'Spiteful and Vindictive' to your list of FAILINGS.*

It is agreed that Mary and Charles should stay with Louisa, and Captain Wentworth is to carry the news to her parents after returning you to Bath. You are sorry to leave Captain Benwick, and as you prepare to take your leave of Lyme he seems on the point of communicating something of particular importance when he is interrupted by Captain Wentworth who urges the necessity of leaving immediately if you are to make it to Bath before dark. You long to know what it is he wishes to tell you, are very sorry for the interruption, and earnestly hope that you will meet Captain Benwick again before too long.

During your journey, Captain Wentworth is silent. Once only, does he exclaim out loud, 'Oh God! That I had not given way to her at the fatal moment! Had I done as I ought! But so eager and so resolute! Dear, sweet Louisa!'

You wonder whether it ever occurs to him now, to question the justness of his own previous opinion as to the universal felicity and advantage of firmness of character; and whether it might not strike him that, like all other qualities of the mind, it should have its proportions and limits. You think it can scarcely escape him to feel that a persuadable temper might sometimes be as much in favour of happiness as a very resolute character.

 Your lack of sympathy for his suffering is astonishingly uncharitable.

 Collect 10 bonus FORTUNE POINTS! Being good only keeps you poor, remember that.

You get on fast and are at Bath by dusk where Captain Wentworth takes leave of you to make the distressing communication to Louisa's parents, before returning to Lyme.

You explain all to your aunt and uncle, who are greatly concerned for Louisa's welfare, and are anxious lest you should have suffered from the distress yourself. You assure them that you are quite well, and are only in need of a little rest. They urge you not to stand on ceremony with them, and you gratefully thank them for their understanding before going to your room and retiring early to bed. Though your mind is full of the events of the past few days, and thoughts of Wentworth and Louisa, you are so fatigued that it is not long before you fall into a deep and uninterrupted sleep.

You receive an encouraging account from Lyme the following afternoon: Louisa shows signs of consciousness and the intervals of sense are longer. Captain Wentworth remains at Lyme and you believe it is only a matter of time before his engagement to Louisa is announced. You steel yourself to receive the news as best you can, and once again immerse yourself wholeheartedly in life at Bath so that you won't have time to reflect on it.

It's unlikely to work. Have 10 INTELLIGENCE POINTS for trying.

To your very great surprise, you find that the very Mr Bennet whom you passed at Lyme has been for some time in Bath, and been so attentive to the Philipses, shown such readiness to apologize for the past, that their former good understanding has been completely re-established and Mr Bennet forgiven completely.

You soon meet Mr Bennet again, and he is greatly surprised to discover that the pretty girl he saw at Lyme is none other than his own cousin. He is quite as good-looking as he appeared at Lyme, his countenance improves by speaking, and his manners are exactly what they ought to be. You converse easily and are delighted with your new acquaintance.

 Collect 40 bonus FORTUNE POINTS.

You could not have supposed it possible that you could feel happy in *anyone's* company so soon after resigning yourself to Wentworth's love for Louisa, let alone the company of a handsome and agreeable gentleman such as Mr Bennet.

 Something is going right for once. It can only be a matter of time before it goes wrong.

Your attachment grows daily; and you are so frequently together, so frequently seen to be pleased with each other, that though you are unaware of it till much later, your perceived intimacy gives rise to the general expectation of an imminent engagement between you. You really do like Mr Bennet, and your attachment advances so rapidly that you do not think it will be long before you are quite in love with him.

 Add 'Ability to Fall in Love Easily and Often' to your list of ACCOMPLISHMENTS.

About this time you receive a letter from Mary which gives you fresh and astonishing news of Louisa. She is well enough recovered to have returned home whither she has gone with Charles, Mary and, to everyone's astonishment, Captain Benwick, who is in love with Louisa and set to marry her before the month is out. You have never in your life been more surprised.

 Didn't take him long to forget about you, did it?

Captain Benwick and Louisa Musgrove! Benwick seemed to prefer *you* when you were at Lyme, but however, that is of no consequence now: Captain Wentworth is free still!

 Just because he's not marrying Louisa, doesn't mean you have any more of a chance with him. You remorselessly broke his heart, remember?

You are once again thrown into a state of turmoil. Having resigned yourself once and for all to a life without Wentworth your mind had naturally directed its thoughts once again to Mr Darcy, and all your tender feelings for that gentleman returned. Then, before you knew it, it was Mr Bennet who occupied all your thoughts. Now you know not what to think. Is it Mr Darcy or Captain Wentworth that you love most? You feel for Captain Wentworth, and hope that he is not suffering too greatly from having lost Louisa; and yet you cannot help but rejoice at the news for your own sake. Though you have tried, it is clear you have not given up hope of regaining Captain Wentworth's heart, and making up for all the past hurt you have been the means of causing.

 Good God, make up your mind, will you?

The following day you are taking a walk about Bath with Mr Bennet when it begins to rain. You turn into a coffee shop, while Mr Bennet goes in search of a carriage. As you sit near the window waiting for him, you discern, most decidedly and distinctly, Captain Wentworth walking down the street. You almost jump in surprise and hope that nobody has perceived you start. As you try to recover your senses, Captain Wentworth enters. He is clearly struck and confused by the sight of you and looks quite red. Mutual enquiries on common subjects are made, but you are both so distracted that neither of you are much the wiser for what you hear. He is much less at ease than formerly; and you cannot help wondering if this consciousness springs from a change in his sentiments towards you.

'Though I came only yesterday,' he says after a short pause, 'I have equipped myself properly for Bath already, you see' (pointing to a new umbrella); 'I wish you would make use of it, if you are determined to walk; though I think it would be more prudent to let me get you a chair.'

 Kind attention from Captain Wentworth is a surprise indeed. Collect 20 CONFIDENCE POINTS and 20 FORTUNE POINTS.

You hurriedly decline it all, sure that the rain will come to nothing in the end, and tell him that you are only waiting for your cousin Mr Bennet to arrive with a carriage.

 Captain Wentworth is finally showing you some attention, and you reject his offer of assistance. What's wrong with you? Deduct 50 INTELLIGENCE POINTS.

311

You have hardly spoken the words when Mr Bennet walks in. In another moment you walk off together, your arm under his, and with a somewhat embarrassed glance you turn back to Captain Wentworth and only have time to bid him good morning. You regret that you were obliged to part with Captain Wentworth so soon, and cannot help wishing Mr Bennet had taken longer in returning. Captain Wentworth's kindness towards you was not unfelt, however, and as the carriage takes you home you feel yourself glowing with the feelings which such attentions naturally excited.

 Collect 50 CONFIDENCE POINTS.

The following evening the Philipses invite you to accompany them to a concert.

> *To accept the invitation, hoping that you'll see Captain Wentworth again, turn to page 318.*
>
> *If you could do with some time to reflect on your feelings for the captain before you see him again, turn to page 277 to stay at home and read instead. You are in a state of turmoil.*

You accept the Philipses' invitation and journey to Bath. You learn that your distant cousins Mary and Charles Musgrove are also in Bath for the season and your aunt Philips encourages you to call on them as soon as possible in the hope that a change of company will help to lift your spirits. You think it highly unlikely, but you have precious few other acquaintances in Bath, so take your aunt's advice and call on the Musgroves.

You're that desperate for friends.

Mary Musgrove is far from beautiful and has none of the Bennet family understanding or temper, but she has a good heart. Her husband Charles does nothing with much zeal except sport, but is civil and agreeable. Charles's attractive but somewhat frivolous sister Louisa is also staying with them for a short while and though their values are on the whole a little too superficial for your liking, you feel that the Musgroves could be a welcome distraction from all unpleasant reflections on Lydia and Wickham's shamefully patched-up marriage, and Darcy's part in it. You have not yet learnt to put from your mind the idea that he did it all for you, but you know it is hardly possible. You therefore vow to forget Mr Darcy and engage wholeheartedly in life at Bath. Time, you hope, will come to heal that particular wound.

It's unlikely.

After the usual enquiries have been made, Louisa proposes a walk to visit the Pump Room and you all readily agree. You have not been there long when Charles begs leave to introduce you to an old friend of his from the navy, by the name of Captain Wentworth. You instantly start, and a deep crimson blush overspreads your features. The gentleman is scarcely more composed and the Musgroves are surprised indeed. They all begin their enquiries and all long to know the meaning of this extraordinary reaction!

'We were acquainted once,' is all the gentleman's reply and you are just able to nod in agreement before hastily making your excuses and leaving the room in search of fresh air.

 Handled THAT well, didn't you? Deduct 10 INTELLIGENCE POINTS.

You have indeed met Captain Wentworth before, and in fact were most intimately acquainted with him just three years ago after meeting him in London with your aunt and uncle Gardiner. Mr Wentworth was a remarkably fine young man, with a great deal of intelligence, spirit and brilliancy and both of you soon fell deeply in love. He proposed and you most happily accepted. Your happiness was but short however.

 As usual.

He had no fortune and no hopes of attaining one but in the most precarious profession of the navy, and Mrs Gardiner strongly objected. Always having had great respect for your aunt's opinion, you were persuaded to believe the engagement a wrong thing and to call it off. You do not blame your aunt for what she did, but you have often wondered whether you might not have been happier with him, no matter what the difficulties, than you have been in sacrificing him.

Clearly, your unhappiness has been entirely your aunt's fault. Deduct 20 INTELLIGENCE POINTS for not blaming her.

Your aunt is evidently very persuasive. Can you claim the same? How would you have reacted in her position? Take the following **Persuasion Test** to see how persuasive YOU are!

Consider the following hypothetical situation: your sister Kitty wants to marry a handsome young sailor who has nothing but himself to recommend him; no hopes of attaining affluence, but in the chances of a most uncertain profession; and no connections to secure even his further rise in that profession.[36]

Do you

a) Let her come to her own decision.

b) Represent to her the arguments against such a connection, reminding her of her claims of birth, beauty and youth, and the uncertainties of the gentleman's profession, but ultimately leave her to make her own decision.

CONTINUED

315

CONTINUED

c) *Deprecate the connection in every light, persuading her to
believe the connection a wrong thing – indiscreet,
improper, hardly capable of success, and not deserving it. Is
your sister, so young, known to so few, to be snatched off
by a stranger without alliance or fortune; or rather sunk by
him into a state of most wearing, anxious, youth-killing
dependence? You think not.*

If you answered a), turn to page 294.

If you answered b), turn to page 329.

If you answered c), turn to page 260.

You make a favourable first impression.

Miss Darcy returns your politeness and likes you a great deal. Though she is amazed to discover just how unaccomplished you are, she admires your spirit and confidence and is warm in her praise of you to her brother.

 Collect 100 FORTUNE POINTS and add 'Miss Darcy' to your list of SUPERIOR CONNECTIONS.

Continue on page 271.

You accept the invitation and you make your way to the concert. As you are waiting in the Octagon Room for some ladies of your aunt's acquaintance, the door opens and Captain Wentworth walks in.

You are very glad you came. Collect 10 FORTUNE POINTS.

He does not look unhappy to see you, and approaches you and begins his polite enquiries.

After talking of the weather, Bath, and the concert, your conversation begins to flag. You are trying to think of something to say when Captain Wentworth, without any introduction, suddenly expresses his surprise at the unexpected engagement between Louisa and Benwick. He can hardly believe that Benwick could so soon have forgotten his late fiancée Fanny Harville, and for a woman such as Louisa. You do not immediately know what to say in reply. You had previously thought Captain Wentworth very much in love with Louisa, but from the way he speaks of her it would seem that his feelings were never that deep. You are pleased to hear it.

Collect 10 CONFIDENCE POINTS.

You had always been rather surprised by the attachment; though Louisa has charms enough, you do not consider depth of feeling and good sense to be among them, and Captain Wentworth always *used* to value good sense above all else – good sense like yours.

Add 'Immodesty' to your list of FAILINGS.

You agree that the engagement was a surprise, and just at that moment, Mr Bennet arrives, and you are necessarily divided from Captain Wentworth for a moment to make your greeting. When you turn back he is gone, and you feel that it is extremely unlucky to have been once again so untimely interrupted by Mr Bennet. Though you know it is unkind, you cannot help somewhat regretting your relation's presence at the concert this evening.

 Serves you right for encouraging his attentions in the first place.

You take your place in the concert room and Mr Bennet sits by you. Towards the close of the first act, in the interval succeeding an Italian song, Mr Bennet asks you to explain the words of the song, but though you do your best, you are a very poor Italian scholar and can only make guesses. As you are trying to make out one of the more difficult words, your attention is suddenly caught by the sight of Captain Wentworth across the room. As your eyes fall on him, his seem to be withdrawn from you. It seems that you were just one moment too late and you regret it heartily.

The performance recommences, and you are obliged to return your gaze forward and at least *appear* to give your attention to the orchestra. When you can next reasonably steal another glance towards Captain Wentworth, he has gone and you cannot make him out amongst the crowd. Mr Bennet leans towards you to whisper more hints and compliments in your ear, and though you enjoyed them once, they can now only distress you. You find that you no longer have any inclination to talk to Mr Bennet and rather wish he was sitting anywhere else but next to you. You had thought yourself almost in love with Mr Bennet, but it dawns on you now that while Captain Wentworth is in the room there can be no thinking of Mr Bennet. Though he has charms enough, there is only one man in the room who could ever make you truly happy. Your attachment to Mr Bennet is entirely over.

 You are fickle and cruel.

The first act finishes and towards the end of the interval you catch sight of Captain Wentworth again. He looks very grave, and only by very slow degrees comes at last near enough to speak to you. His manner is so greatly changed that you feel there must be something the matter and long to know what it is. He begins by speaking of the concert and it is only your defence of the performance that at last improves his countenance a little. He even goes so far as to look down towards the bench, as if about to sit down; but at that very moment Mr Bennet begs your pardon, but you 'must be applied to etc.' to explain Italian again.

 His timing is incredible. Deduct 50 FORTUNE POINTS.

It is all you can do to contain your ill-will towards Mr Bennet for this third untimely interruption, and you begin to wonder whether they are 'accidental' after all, or whether Mr Bennet rather feels your preference for Captain Wentworth and wishes to recover your attention.

You hastily do your best to explain the words to Mr Bennet, though you really don't know what they mean, and when you turn again to Captain Wentworth he makes a hurried sort of farewell, insisting that he must get home as fast as he can.

'Is not this song worth staying for?' you say, anxious for him not to leave so soon.

'No!' he replies impressively, 'there is nothing worth my staying for,' and he is gone directly.

Oh dear. Deduct 50 CONFIDENCE POINTS and 50 FORTUNE POINTS.

You are struck by his angry tone and cannot immediately account for it. And then all at once it occurs to you: Captain Wentworth is jealous of Mr Bennet! It is the only intelligible motive.

Either that or he really doesn't like you.

Captain Wentworth is jealous of your affection and for a moment the gratification is exquisite indeed. But, very different thoughts quickly succeed. How is the truth to reach him that you feel nothing for Mr Bennet? It is misery to think of your cousin's attentions now; their evil is incalculable.

Deduct 20 FORTUNE POINTS. You are not so sure Mr Bennet counts as a SUPERIOR CONNECTION after all.

The following day you are engaged to visit an old childhood friend by the name of Mrs Smith, who now permanently resides in Bath. She has heard rumours that you are soon to be engaged to Mr Bennet and when you assure her that there is no foundation to them she is most heartily relieved. You are shocked to learn that Mr Bennet, far from being rich, has been cut off by his father, is in great debt, and seeks to marry his way into solvency again.

 Duped. Again!

Though you are far from rich yourself, by marrying you he would integrate himself once more within the Bennet family, by which means he hopes to appease his father and reclaim the fortune due to him, and the entail of the Longbourn estate which is, in fact, his by rights. You thank her most gratefully for the information, and chide yourself for being seduced by his flattery. You have now an even greater reason to regret the attentions which are threatening to ruin, once again (and perhaps for evermore), your hopes with Captain Wentworth.

 Strike 'Mr Bennet' from your list of SUPERIOR CONNECTIONS immediately, and add him to your list of INFERIOR CONNECTIONS. Knowing him is really ruining things for you right now.

The next morning, before you have a chance to tell your aunt and uncle the truth about Mr Bennet, you are distracted by the arrival in Bath of your cousins Charles and Mary Musgrove, and the Harvilles from Lyme. You are obliged to be with the Musgroves from breakfast to dinner and when you arrive you find that Captain Wentworth is also with them. When he sees you, he looks as grave as he did when he left the concert and just two minutes after your entering the room, he turns to Captain

Harville and says, 'We will write the letter we were talking of, Harville, now, if you will give me materials.'

It seems he will do anything to avoid talking to you.

Deduct 50 CONFIDENCE POINTS.

The materials are all at hand on a separate table which Captain Wentworth makes his way to and, nearly turning his back on you all, sits down and is engrossed by writing.

While the others all talk gaily of Louisa and Benwick's forthcoming marriage, Captain Harville leaves his seat and, moving to a window, invites you to join him. He shows you a small miniature painting of Captain Benwick, which you guess is to be for Louisa, but which, he tells you in a deep tone, was originally done for his poor sister Fanny. Captain Harville was unable to bear the heartache of getting it set for another, so instead Captain Wentworth has undertaken the charge, and is at this very moment writing the letter of instruction for it.

'Poor Fanny!' adds Captain Harville with a quivering lip. 'She would not have forgotten him so soon! It was not in her nature. She doted on him.'

'It would not be in the nature of any woman who truly loved,' you reply with meaning.

Captain Harville smiles, as much as to say, 'Do you claim that for your sex?' and your feelings for Captain Wentworth are uppermost in your mind as you go on:

'We certainly do not forget you so soon as you forget us. We cannot help ourselves. We live at home, quiet, confined, and our feelings prey upon us. You are forced on exertion. You have always a profession, pursuits, business of some sort or other, to take you back into the world immediately, and continual occupation and change soon weaken impressions.'

Captain Harville smiles and observes to you that he has never in his life opened a book which didn't have something to say about woman's inconstancy. You are not impressed with this argument.

 Collect 20 INTELLIGENCE POINTS.

'Yes, but they were all written by men!' you retort. 'Men have had every advantage of us in telling their own story. Education has been theirs in so much higher a degree; the pen has been in their hands. I will not allow books to prove anything.'

 You deserve 50 FORTUNE POINTS *for that one.*

'We shall never agree upon this question,' Captain Harville begins to say, when a slight noise calls your attention to Captain Wentworth. It is nothing more than that his pen has fallen down; but you are half inclined to suspect that the pen only fell because he was occupied by you, and striving to catch sounds. You cannot deny that there is part of you that hopes he *did* hear you, though you cannot imagine it possible from such a distance.

You turn your attention back to Captain Harville and assure him that you believe men such as him to be capable of everything great and good in their married lives, so long as the woman they love lives, and lives for them. The only unenviable privilege you claim for your own sex is that of loving longest, when existence or when hope is gone.

'You are a good soul,' cries Captain Harville, putting his hand on your arm, quite affectionately. 'There is no quarrelling with you. And when I think of Benwick, my tongue is tied.'

If anyone can be said to have won this argument, it's you.
Collect 20 INTELLIGENCE POINTS.

At that moment you are interrupted by the arrival of Captain Benwick himself, accompanied by Louisa and her parents. They have come for the Harvilles whom they wish to take on a tour of their favourite spots in Bath. You are all to meet again this evening, and Louisa and Captain Benwick express their pleasure at the prospect of having a greater opportunity to talk to you once again and catch up on all that has passed since you were last together, at Lyme. The Harvilles are ready to go and are only waiting on Captain Wentworth, who seals his letter with great rapidity, and is then ready. It seems to you that he even has a hurried, agitated air, which shows impatience to be gone, as if not wishing to be left alone with only you and the Musgroves. You have the kindest 'Good morning, God bless you!' from Captain Harville, but not a word, nor even a *look*, from Captain Wentworth.

Oh dear. Your CONFIDENCE drops by a full 100 points.

You turn towards the table where he has been writing so as to conceal your disappointed expression from the Musgroves and are endeavouring to recover your spirits when you hear footsteps returning. The door opens, and Captain Wentworth himself comes back into the room. He begs your pardon, but he forgot his gloves, and he instantly crosses the room to the writing table, draws out a letter from under the scattered paper, places it before you, looks at you with eyes of entreaty for a time, before hastily collecting his gloves, and once again leaving the room.

You are astonished indeed: while writing his letter of instruction, it seems he was also addressing *you*.

 Better have 50 CONFIDENCE POINTS back.

You hastily open the letter with trembling hands and your eyes devour his words. He has been listening to you and Captain Harville half in agony and half in hope. He prays that he is not too late, and offers himself to you again with a heart even more your own than when you almost broke it, three years ago. He has loved none but you – unjust he has been, weak and resentful too, but never inconstant – and you alone have brought him back to Bath. Uncertain of his fate, he will return to the Musgroves' lodgings as soon as possible and 'A word, a look,' he concludes, 'will be enough to decide whether I will see you again this evening or never.'

 Have another 50 CONFIDENCE POINTS back and collect 100 FORTUNE POINTS.

You are overwhelmed with surprise and happiness and go after the captain at once.

 You catch up with the captain who, for the second time in his life, makes you a proposal of marriage.

If you wish to accept, you'll need to check your
INTELLIGENCE SCORE.

If it's 450 or above, turn to page 290.

If it's below 450, turn to page 293.

Alternatively, if it suddenly dawns on you that though you
have always secretly loved Captain Wentworth and longed
for him to forgive you, in actual fact all you really wanted
was his forgiveness and besides you are not sure that you
could really bear the anxiety that would come with being
married to a captain of the navy, then turn to page 288 to
do your best to get out of a truly awkward situation.

You politely turn down the Philipses' invitation, and settle back into everyday life at Longbourn. You do your best to forget Mr Darcy, but after learning what he has done for Lydia and Wickham, that is easier said than done.

Congratulations! You have completed Stage Four.

Will this ever end?

Turn to page 333 to find out.

b) Represent to Kitty the arguments against such a connection,
but ultimately leave her to make her own decision.

Your Persuasive skills need more work. Remember that you are always right, and endeavour to force your opinion on others more often.

Continue on page 296.

You gratefully accept Mr Bennet and do your best to forget Captain Wentworth and Mr Darcy. Your mother and sisters will be grateful, you are sure. You write to Jane the following day to tell her the news, and she is extremely delighted for you. Mr Bennet goes to visit your father to ask for your hand formally and it is soon all arranged so that you are married in Hertfordshire before the month is out. It is not until the day following the ceremony, however, that you discover that Mr Bennet is heavily in debt, has a serious gambling addiction, no career prospects and does not love you at all. The sole reason he attached himself to you was to get hold of what little money your father could lay upon you and the promise of the Longbourn estate when your father dies. You have all been sorely deceived and you are utterly devastated.

The End

Dear, oh dear, oh dear. This match was neither loving nor prudent despite appearances to the contrary. What a mug! You have failed to complete your mission.

You have made a terrible first impression and are going to have to work extremely hard to undo the damage.

Miss Darcy thinks you horribly reserved, cold and proud. Though she is outwardly warm and friendly, she cannot like you, and influences her brother against you whenever she can.

 Deduct 100 INTELLIGENCE POINTS.

Continue on page 271.

STAGE FIVE

BOUT THIS TIME, your mother's mind is opened again to the agitation of hope, by an article of news which had now begun to circulate: the housekeeper at Netherfield has received orders to prepare for the arrival of her master, who is coming down in a day or two, to shoot there for several weeks.

Oh Lord. Here we go again.

Jane is unable to hear of Bingley's coming without changing colour, though she assures you later that she has long since given up all feelings of attachment to him.

Mr Bingley comes at last, and on the third morning after his arrival in Hertfordshire, your mother spies him from her dressing-room window entering the paddock and riding towards the house – with Mr Darcy. Your astonishment at Darcy's coming – at his coming to Netherfield, to Longbourn, and voluntarily seeking you again even though Lydia is now married, at Darcy's own expense, to his greatest enemy, Mr Wickham – is almost equal to what you had known on first witnessing his altered behaviour in Derbyshire.

You sit intently at work, striving to be composed, and not daring to lift up your eyes. On the gentlemen's appearing, Jane's colour increases; yet she receives them with tolerable ease. You say as little to either as civility allows, and sit down again to your work with an eagerness which it does not often command.

Add 'Slacker' to your list of FAILINGS.

You venture only one glance at Darcy. He looks serious as usual, and, you think, more as he used to look in Hertfordshire, than as you saw him at Pemberley. More reserve, and less anxiety to please than when you last met are plainly expressed. You are disappointed, and angry with yourself for being so.

'Could I expect it to be otherwise!' you say to yourself. 'Yet why did he come?'

Your mother is over-polite to Mr Bingley and, to your great shame, pointedly rude to Mr Darcy. She gloats over the marriage of Lydia but laments that she must live so far away, and you are in agonies at your mother's rudeness.

 Deduct 20 FORTUNE POINTS and 20 CONFIDENCE POINTS.

At this moment you feel that years of happiness cannot make amends to you or Jane for the many times she has embarrassed you like this.

When the gentlemen rise to go away, your mother invites them to dine at Longbourn in a few days' time. They assent, and then leave your party.

As soon as they are gone you walk out to recover your spirits; or rather to dwell without interruption on those subjects that must deaden them more.

 OK. That's it. Deduct 200 INTELLIGENCE POINTS.

Mr Darcy's behaviour astonishes and vexes you.

'Why, if he came only to be silent, grave, and indifferent,' you say, 'did he come at all? He could be still amiable, still pleasing to my uncle and aunt, when he was in town; and why not to me? If he fears me, why come hither? If he no longer cares for me, why silent? Teasing, teasing, man! I will think no more about him.'

 Deduct 20 INTELLIGENCE POINTS for once again vowing to forget Mr Darcy when you know there's absolutely no chance of that ever happening.

On Tuesday a large party is assembled at Longbourn; and Bingley and Darcy arrive in very good time. Bingley hesitantly takes his place next to Jane but Mr Darcy is almost as far from you as the table can divide you.

 Deduct 40 FORTUNE POINTS.

You hope that the evening will afford some opportunity of bringing you together; and when the gentlemen finally join you in the drawing room you think he looks as if he will answer your hopes; but everything is overthrown when your mother loudly insists that he join her table for a hand of whist.

 Deduct another 40 FORTUNE POINTS.

Every expectation of pleasure is immediately lost, and once again you find yourself blaming your mother for your present unhappiness! You and Darcy are confined to your different tables for the rest of the evening, and the only hope you have left is that his eyes are so often turned towards your side of the room as yours are to his, that he plays as unsuccessfully as yourself.

Your mother is in very great spirits at the end of the evening, so much so that she is quite disappointed at not seeing Mr

Bingley again the next day to make his proposal to Jane. A few days later Mr Bingley calls again, however, but this time alone. You try not to feel disappointed.

But you are. Deduct 20 CONFIDENCE POINTS.

Bingley scarcely needs an invitation to stay to supper; and before he goes away, an engagement is formed, chiefly through his own and your mother's means, for his coming the next morning to shoot with your father.

Bingley is punctual to his appointment and after the shooting, returns to dinner. His attentions to Jane give you great pleasure and he seems, if possible, more in love with her than he was when he was last at Netherfield. That evening you have a letter to write and go into the breakfast room for that purpose soon after tea. On returning to the drawing room when your letter is finished, you see, to your infinite surprise, your sister and Bingley standing together over the hearth as if engaged in earnest conversation. Had this led to no suspicion, the faces of both as they hastily turn round and move away from each other, would have told it all. Not a syllable is uttered by either; and you are on the point of going away again, when Bingley, whispering a few words to your sister, runs out of the room.

Instantly embracing you, Jane acknowledges with the liveliest emotion that she is the happiest creature in the world.

Finally, some good FORTUNE (for one of you at least). Collect 10 FORTUNE POINTS.

'I am certainly the most fortunate creature that ever existed!' she cries. 'Oh! Lizzy, why am I thus singled from my family, and blessed above them all! If I could but see *you* as happy! If there *were* but such another man for you!'

 That's it, Jane, rub it in.

She goes instantly to your mother, and you are left to smile at the rapidity and ease with which an affair that has given you so many months of suspense and vexation is finally settled.

 You are saved from homelessness. Collect 50 FORTUNE POINTS.

 You are still single. Deduct 100 CONFIDENCE POINTS.

One morning, about a week after Bingley's engagement to Jane, you receive a very unexpected visitor in the name of Lady Catherine de Bourgh. Your astonishment is beyond words.

She enters the room with an air more than usually ungracious, makes no other reply to your salutation than a slight inclination of the head, and sits down without saying a word. Your mother, with great civility, begs her ladyship to take some refreshment; but Lady Catherine very resolutely, and not very politely, declines eating anything; and then, rising up, asks you to show her the little copse on the other side of your lawn.

 This ought to be fun...

You obey, and as soon as you enter the copse, Lady Catherine begins by declaring that you can be at no loss to understand the reason of her journey. You reply, with unaffected astonishment, that you have not the least idea why she has paid you the honour of visiting, and from her furious expression you quickly see that this was not the answer she wanted to hear.

'A report of a most alarming nature reached me two days ago,' she says in an angry tone. 'I was told that not only your sister was on the point of being most advantageously married, but that *you*, that Miss Elizabeth Bennet, would in all likelihood be soon afterwards united to my nephew Mr Darcy.'

You are once again genuinely astonished. You know not what to think and your spirits are thrown into discomposure.

'Though I *know* it must be a scandalous falsehood...' continues Lady Catherine, 'I instantly resolved on setting off for this place, that I might make my sentiments known to you.'

Your nerves are greatly agitated, both by Lady Catherine's tone, and the idea that such a report could be in existence at all. Who could have started it? Could it have in some way come from Darcy himself? You can scarcely allow yourself to consider it a possibility and instantly banish the thought from your mind.

But not before collecting 50 CONFIDENCE POINTS.

You direct your attention back to Lady Catherine and tell her that her coming to Longbourn will only be a confirmation of the report if, indeed, such a report exists.

'This is not to be borne!' cries Lady Catherine. 'Miss Bennet, do you know who I am? Let me be rightly understood. Mr Darcy is engaged to *my daughter*.'

You wonder how she could suppose that Darcy would make a proposal to you if he really is engaged to Miss de Bourgh.

'My daughter and my nephew are destined for each other by the voice of every member of their respective houses,' she continues, 'and what is to divide them? The upstart pretensions of a young woman without family, connections, or fortune?'

Being reminded of your pitiful situation is the last thing you need. Deduct 50 CONFIDENCE POINTS.

It is with great difficulty that you are able to contain your indignation.

'Whatever my connections may be,' you reply as coolly as you can, 'if your nephew does not object to them, they can be nothing to you.'

She asks you directly if you are engaged to him, and though you would rather not, for the mere purpose of obliging Lady Catherine, answer this question, you cannot but say after a moment's deliberation, 'I am not.'

Lady Catherine seems pleased, which only riles you further. 'And will you promise me never to enter into such an engagement?' she asks.

You will make her no promise of the kind and tell her that she has widely mistaken your character if she thinks you can be worked on by such persuasions as hers. You beg, therefore, to be importuned no further on the subject, and turn back towards the house.

'Not so hasty, if you please,' she insists, stopping you before you can get away. 'I have by no means done, I have still another objection to add. I am no stranger to the particulars of your youngest sister's infamous elopement and patched-up marriage. Is *such* a girl to be my nephew's sister? Heaven and earth – are the shades of Pemberley to be thus polluted?'

You know that Lydia's elopement has ruined, forever, any hope of a renewal of Darcy's attentions to you, and you do not need to be reminded of it by Lady Catherine.

Deduct 40 FORTUNE POINTS and 40 CONFIDENCE POINTS.

'You can *now* have nothing further to say,' you resentfully answer. 'You have insulted me in every possible method; I must beg to return to the house. I have nothing further to say; you know my sentiments.'

You reach the door of her carriage, when, turning hastily round, Lady Catherine concludes, 'I take no leave of you, Miss Bennet. I send no compliments to your mother. You deserve no such attention. I am most seriously displeased.'

You make no answer, and, without attempting to persuade her ladyship to return to the house, walk quietly into it yourself.

The discomposure of spirits which this extraordinary visit throws you into cannot be easily overcome, and it is many hours before you can think of it less than incessantly. From what the report of your engagement can originate, you are at a loss to imagine except perhaps the fact that the marriage of Jane and Bingley will bring you and Darcy more frequently together.

Nevertheless, it has raised your hopes. Collect 50 CONFIDENCE POINTS.

———⚬———

A few days after Lady Catherine's visit, Mr Bingley once again brings Mr Darcy with him to Longbourn. The gentlemen arrive early; and before your mother has time to tell Mr Darcy of your having seen his aunt – of which you sit in momentary dread – Bingley, who wants to be alone with Jane, proposes your all walking out. It is immediately agreed to, to your own great relief: your mother is not in the habit of walking and will therefore have no further opportunity to embarrass you. Your sister Mary can never spare time for walking, but the remaining five of you set off together. Bingley and Jane soon allow the rest of you to outstrip them and lag behind, while you, Kitty, and Darcy are left to entertain each other. Very little is said by any of you: Kitty is too much afraid of him to talk; you are secretly forming a desperate resolution to thank him for what he did for Lydia; and what Darcy's own reasons for silence are you dread to think.

Kitty wishes to call on Maria and so the three of you walk in the direction of Lucas Lodge. As you see no occasion for making it a general concern, when Kitty leaves, you go boldly on with him alone. Now is the moment for your resolution to be executed and, while your courage is high, you thank him for his unexampled kindness to your poor sister.

'I am sorry, exceedingly sorry,' replies Darcy, in a tone of surprise and emotion, 'that you have ever been informed of what may, in a mistaken light, have given you uneasiness. I did not think Mrs Gardiner was so little to be trusted.'

 It had to backfire somehow, didn't it?

You are anxious for him not to think ill of your aunt and hastily explain that it was Lydia's thoughtlessness that first betrayed to you that Darcy had been concerned in the matter, and that you only applied to Mrs Gardiner because you could not rest till you knew the particulars. You thank him again and again, in the name of all your family, for his generous compassion.

'If you will thank me,' he replies, 'let it be for yourself alone. I shall not attempt to deny that the wish of giving you happiness added to my other inducements to act. But your family owes me nothing. Much as I respect them, I believe I thought only of you.'

You are so very surprised at this unexpected turn of events, and so overwhelmed with emotion by what you have heard, that for some moments you are too embarrassed to say a word. After a short pause, your companion adds, 'You are too generous to trifle with me. If your feelings are still what they were last April, tell me so at once. My affections and wishes are unchanged; but one word from you will silence me on this subject forever.'

 This is the moment you've been waiting for.

 It is time to add up all your scores: your FORTUNE SCORE, your CONFIDENCE SCORE, your INTELLIGENCE SCORE, your CONNECTIONS SCORE, and your overall ACCOMPLISHMENTS SCORE.

OK?

Now, turn to page 349.

You try not to worry about it and do your best to get back to sleep. At last you are successful and you wake in the morning as happy as you were when you first took to your bed, and not even your mother can have any effect on your high spirits.

When you next see Mr Darcy you ask him playfully to account for his ever having fallen in love with you.

'My beauty you had early withstood, and as for my manners – my behaviour to *you* was at least always bordering on the uncivil, and I never spoke to you without rather wishing to give you pain than not. Now be sincere; did you admire me for my impertinence?'

'For the liveliness of your mind, I did,' replies your husband-to-be.

And so it continues, each of you light-heartedly teasing the other. You have a joint wedding with your sister Jane and happy is the day on which your mother gets rid of her two most deserving daughters. With what delighted pride she afterwards visits Mrs Bingley and talks of Mrs Darcy may be guessed. Mr Bingley buys an estate in the neighbouring county to Derbyshire and you and Jane, in addition to every other source of happiness, are within thirty miles of each other. You invite Kitty to stay with you often, and in society so superior to what she had generally known, her improvement is great. Mary stays at home and when no longer mortified by comparisons between her sisters' beauty and her own, mixes more with the world than she was wont. Though Wickham can never be received at Pemberley, for your sake, Mr Darcy assists him further in his profession, and Lydia is an occasional visitor when her husband is away enjoying himself in London or Bath.

Miss Bingley is deeply mortified by Darcy's marriage, but as she thinks it advisable to retain the right of visiting Pemberley, she drops all her resentment, is fonder than ever of Georgiana and endeavours to make up for all prior incivility to you.

Lady Catherine, having been extremely indignant when she first learnt of your engagement, sends a letter so very abusive, especially of you, that at first all intercourse is put to an end. At length, you persuade your husband to overlook the offence and seek a reconciliation. At last her resentment gives way and either out of affection for him, or curiosity to see how you conduct yourself, she condescends to wait on you at Pemberley, in spite of the pollution which its woods have received, not merely from the presence of such a mistress as yourself, but the visits of all your inferior connections.

With the Gardiners you are always on the most intimate terms and both you and Mr Darcy feel the warmest gratitude towards them as the persons who, by bringing you into Derbyshire, were the means of uniting you at last.

THE END

Congratulations.

You have successfully completed your mission.

Feeling all the more than common awkwardness and anxiety of his situation, you are now forced to speak yourself; and immediately, though not very fluently, give him to understand that your sentiments have undergone so material a change since the period to which he alludes, as to make you receive with gratitude and pleasure his present assurances. You can barely meet his eye, but when you do, you see that the expression of heartfelt delight which diffuses his face becomes him exceedingly well. You listen in a quiet ecstasy as he tells you of feelings which, in proving of what importance you are to him, make his affection every moment more valuable.

You walk on, without knowing in what direction. There is too much to be thought, and felt, and said, for attention to any other objects. You talk over every past misunderstanding and the circumstances which led to your respective changes in opinion of each other and walk together happily till the time calls you back indoors.

The news shocks your family greatly. Jane is worried that you do not really love him, your mother is delighted at how rich you'll be, and your father is incredulous. At length, by repeated assurances that Mr Darcy is really the object of your choice, and by explaining the gradual change which your estimation of him has undergone, relating your absolute certainty that his affection is not the work of a day, but has stood the test of many months' suspense, you conquer your father's incredulity, and reconcile him to the match. You retire to bed that evening perhaps even more happy than Jane, and soon fall into a deep and blissful sleep.

It is a great surprise to you therefore when you wake suddenly in the middle of the night, your heart beating at your chest and a cold sweat on your brow. You feel a deep knot of anxiety within you. What could possibly be wrong? The man of your dreams wants to marry you and nothing stands in your way. Just hours before, you were the happiest woman alive; now you feel sick with worry. There is something troubling you, but you know not what it could be. A bad dream perhaps? All you have is an impression of a feeling, a deep uneasiness that you cannot immediately explain.

 It's time to check your INTELLIGENCE SCORE.

If it is below 400, turn to page 345.

If it is 400 or above, turn to page 350.

Your FORTUNE SCORE might be pitifully low; you have barely any SUPERIOR CONNECTIONS; your CONFIDENCE SCORE is bound to be mediocre; your INTELLIGENCE SCORE is undoubtedly passable but unlikely to be anything more; it's unlikely that you boast any real ACCOMPLISHMENTS...

BUT

Mr Darcy doesn't mind!

He is willing to marry you anyway, despite your many, MANY FAILINGS.

It's your lucky day.

Continue on page 347.

You rise from your bed and go to the window, in the hope that you will be able to clear your mind. It is dark, but the grey light from the moon illuminates the garden. All is still, all is peaceful. Your mind, by contrast, is in turmoil. You try to gather your thoughts, but you cannot. Why, if you are happy, do you feel so ill at ease? The only man on earth who could make you happy has said he wants to marry you, and you have accepted him. Everything is set for your happiness if only you could submit to it. You want so desperately to do so, and yet you know there is something wrong. You try to comfort yourself, to imagine your future life of happiness with Mr Darcy, but though you foresee happiness in the months immediately ahead, your confidence falters when you try to look beyond them. Pemberley is beautiful, no doubt, and your husband-to-be quite the most remarkable man you've ever met; your library will be vast and diverting – but something about this picture does not sit comfortably.

Just what on earth are you going to do with your days once you're married? What will you and your husband talk about? Will you forever be going over the unlikely circumstances under which you met and (at last) fell in love? Will you go on reminding one another of how it was in the beginning until long after you have ceased to feel anything but indifference for each other? Familiarity breeds contempt, and Pemberley is a long way from Hertfordshire; who can say how often your friends and family will be able to visit you and diversify the domestic scene? You reassure yourself that even if these fears are just, before long, perhaps, you will have children, and their care will sufficiently divert you. You take comfort in this, until a vision of your mother comes before you, and you feel that to live solely for your children is no life at all. God forbid you should turn out like your mother.

You tell yourself these doubts are only natural and dismiss them as best you can, but still your mind is ill at ease. Something deeper is yet troubling you, but still you know not what it is. Could it have been something you read? With little hope of finding an answer there, but at a loss for what else to do, you make your way down to the library. In the light afforded you by your low-burning candle you scan the shelves for those titles you read most recently, and take down a number of volumes. You flick through the first that comes to hand, hoping to find something that will prompt your memory and bring to the fore that which yet lingers at the back of your mind; but no such discovery befriends you. You take up a second volume, and a third, desperately searching your mind, trying to think what it might be that could have remained with you on some deep level, though you were not at first aware of it. Still you find nothing. You go back to the shelves and take down volume after volume – all your favourite novels, all those works which you have treasured over these last years – until you are surrounded by a sea of books, spread out around you as you sit on the library floor in the quiet of the half-light.

You are still for some moments, unsure of what to do. And slowly at first, but then all at once, it begins to dawn on you. A wave of realization washes over you with the most awful force. You take up the book nearest to hand and skip to the end, to those most treasured passages where the heroine is finally united with the man she loves. He makes her a proposal of marriage, she accepts it, and the story ends happily. You pick up another title. The same is true here. You hastily take up volume after volume only to discover the same devastating truth in all of them: the moment the heroine of the narrative agrees to wed, the book comes to a swift end. Following every happy marriage are the words 'The End', stamped most authoritatively upon the page.

'Good God!' you think to yourself, 'And is this the fate that awaits me also? If I marry Mr Darcy, will I too, face "The End"?' Apparently there is nothing that can follow the marriages of your favourite heroines – no story worth telling, no circumstance worth reading; all is apparently devoid of interest. Their adventure and excitement are over; they cease to be of interest to anyone.

A thousand feelings rush upon you at once, and your world seems to close in around you. What you stand to gain upon your marriage to Mr Darcy is great indeed, but what must you sacrifice? What must be given up for this match to take place? Not just your name, but your very *existence* as Elizabeth Bennet. Every book that surrounds you seems to be forcing you to the same conclusion, the same distressing realization: that marriage will be 'The End' for you. Are you ready for it? Are you ready for the end of the adventure – ready to say goodbye to all in life that might be worth writing or reading about?

Never before have you been so distraught, so torn, so at a loss. What is to be your fate? You must make the final choice, the choice of all choices. Are you prepared to sign yourself over to this new life, to disappear from notice, to cease to be of interest, to cease to be Elizabeth Bennet and become, instead, Mrs Darcy?

The shock of your realization is great, and you know not how many hours you sit there in the darkness amongst your books (your candle long since burnt out) before at last climbing heavily and wearily back to your bed to steal what repose you can before the new day begins.

When you awake but a few hours later, it is with a very heavy feeling. Jane's shock at your distressed appearance is great. Through many tears, and with great difficulty, you tell her that you cannot, you must not marry Mr Darcy. Though he is the man most likely to bring you happiness of any man you are ever likely to meet, you must give him up; another fate awaits you. You know not how the news is to be broken to him, but know you cannot see him yourself. To be the cause of so much distress to him is almost enough to break your heart entirely and you do not have the strength for it.

Jane arranges it all. You are to be conveyed by your father's carriage to London, to your aunt, your dear aunt Gardiner, to whom she sends word by the first morning's post. All is commotion at Longbourn. Your father is perplexed and concerned, your mother is distracted. That you could have secured the hand of the richest man of your acquaintance only to throw it away again the next day seems to her the most wilful obstinacy, and she immediately takes to her bed in a fit of nerves. It is left to Jane to take the news to Mr Darcy, and with the help of Mr Bingley the deed is done while you are already on your way to London. You know not what grief he feels on the occasion for you never ask Jane, and the matter is never spoken of between you again.

You arrive in London, and your sister's letter having only just preceded you, are welcomed into the arms of your aunt who mercifully spares you questions. You talk and eat but little that night, and are grateful for the silent understanding shown to you by your aunt and uncle. You do little more than rest in your first weeks there, but you know that in time your spirits will be restored. You know what you must do, and as the pain begins to subside, your strength grows. Agonizing though it was, you *know* you made the right decision and this conviction supports you through the darkest hours.

You alone know it at present, but the night you spent amongst your books was significant for more than one reason: you knew soon enough that you could never marry Mr Darcy, but with this surprising discovery came a second realization, no less startling than the first, and you knew there and then what you must do instead. That night, you realized that you *yourself* must write.

On the Monday morning of your sixth week at Gracechurch Street you wake with a strong sense of purpose. After breakfast, you make your excuses and go to the drawing room. You sit down at the writing table, draw out a pen and a blank sheet of paper, and prepare to write the first page of your book. Drawing heavily on your own experiences over these last few years, you plan to write about the adventures of a young woman in pursuit of the right match. Unlike the volumes that lay before you that fateful night however, *your* book will not send out the message that Woman's only choice is to marry – and that her story will end the moment she does so. You are determined to find a way for your heroine to say 'no' to 'The End' and continue her adventure. You dip your pen in your ink, put pen to paper and begin to write as follows:

Continue on page ix.

NOTES

1   Henry Crawford is a character from *Mansfield Park*, and this diversion plays on events that happen in that book.

2   This diversion is taken from *Love and Freindship* [sic], one of Austen's juvenilia works. Willoughby and Wickham both play similar roles in the novels from which they come, so there is a little play on that here too since Mr W could refer to either one of them, depending on which route you took to get to this page. There is also a reference to *Emma* here, in which Mrs Elton refers to her husband as 'Mr E'; Emma considers this to be extremely vulgar.

3   This short diversion is taken from *Emma* (Volume III, chapter iii).

4   The conjecture as to what Mr Darcy might have to say about Gracechurch Street is from *Pride and Prejudice* (Volume II, chapter ii), where Lizzy and Mrs Gardiner discuss the unlikelihood of Jane meeting Mr Bingley in London unless he comes to visit her at the Gardiners' house. As Lizzy says, '*That* is quite impossible; for now he is in the custody of his friend, and Mr Darcy would no more suffer him to call on Jane in such a part of London! ... Mr Darcy may perhaps have *heard* of such a place as Gracechurch Street ...'

5   The main storyline of this diversion is taken from *Sense and Sensibility*.

6   In *Emma*, Jane Fairfax almost takes up a position as a governess and, judging by how ill she gets at the mere thought of it, this is apparently a fate worse than death.

7   The Boulanger is the only dance mentioned by name in Austen's work. Mr Bingley dances it at the first Meryton assembly in *Pride and Prejudice*, as Mrs Bennet is so kind as to point out in her detailed report to her husband (Volume I, chapter iii).

8 *Fordyce's Sermons* is the text Mr Collins chooses to read aloud after his first dinner at Longbourn in *Pride and Prejudice* (Volume I, chapter xiv). Judging by Lydia's reaction (she 'gapes' and interrupts him to give Mrs Bennet some gossip about the officers) it is incredibly boring and it is easy to imagine him torturing his unlucky wife with nightly readings. It is therefore an excellent and appropriate weapon with which to finally exact revenge and dispatch him.

9 The room you find yourself in here is a reference to both the 'white attic' and the 'East Room' of *Mansfield Park*, in which Fanny Price sleeps and keeps most of her possessions, respectively.

10 The mysterious girl's dialogue about her room, beginning, 'I am sorry there is no fire…' is taken directly from *Mansfield Park*.

11 The mad girl in the attic mentions Catherine Morland who is, of course, the original heroine of *Northanger Abbey*, from which this overall diversion is taken. She also mentions Elinor Dashwood, who is a character from *Sense and Sensibility*. These comments playfully reference the fact that, in this book, both women have been displaced from their narratives by Elizabeth Bennet.

12 In a letter to her niece Fanny Knight, dated 18 November 1814, Jane Austen writes, 'anything is to be preferred or endured rather than marrying without affection,' and if you choose to reject Mr Collins's proposal, that is probably your view too.

13 The obstacles that stand in the way of Elizabeth and Tom are the same as those that would have prevented the real Tom Lefroy from ever proposing to Jane Austen, and are quoted directly from Claire Tomalin's biography, *Jane Austen, A Life* (Penguin, London, 2000), p. 121.

14 This diversion borrows from the point at which, in *Northanger Abbey*, Catherine Morland meets Henry Tilney for the first time in Bath. Tom Lefroy is a young Irishman who Austen met, and most likely fell in love with, in 1796. For more details see *Jane Austen, A Life*, Claire Tomalin (Penguin, London, 2000). Their meeting is also the subject of the 2007 film *Becoming Jane*.

15 The real Tom Lefroy married a wealthy heiress from Wexford.

16   Tom's opinion that there has not been a decent novel released since *Tom Jones* is taken from Austen's letter to her sister, Cassandra (Saturday, 9 January 1796), in which she tells her that Mr Lefroy is 'a great admirer of Tom Jones'.

17   The line 'I mean to confine myself in future to Mr Tom Lefroy, for whom I do not care sixpence' is taken from the letter detailed above.

18   Elizabeth's dialogue, beginning 'I am almost afraid to tell you how my Irish friend and I behaved,' is taken from the letter detailed above.

19   The main storyline of this diversion is taken from *Northanger Abbey*.

20   You are lucky enough to join Henry Tilney in his curricle – a smart, chariot-style, two-wheeled vehicle.

21   In *Sense and Sensibility* (Volume I, chapter xviii), Edward Ferrars gives his view on the picturesque. Were he to take this test, he would probably choose option a), which is largely lifted from what he has to say on the matter.

22   In *Northanger Abbey* (Volume I, chapter xiv), we are told that 'Catherine was so hopeful a scholar [of the picturesque] that when they gained the top of Beechen Cliff, she voluntarily rejected the whole city of Bath as unworthy to make part of a landscape.' It is very likely therefore that, were she to take this test, she would choose option c).

23   The idea that you might prefer to 'work for your bread than marry' any member of the Darcy family is taken from *Lady Susan*.

24   In order to explain why Elizabeth is not better acquainted with the Woodhouses I have borrowed from *Persuasion*, in which the Elliots let Kellynch Hall to Admiral and Mrs Croft.

25   In this diversion you meet Emma Woodhouse who is, of course, the original heroine of *Emma* from which the storyline of this overall diversion is taken.

26   Mr Darcy's farmer is described here as 'a very plain man, remarkably plain, but that is nothing compared with his entire want of gentility'. This is Emma Woodhouse's opinion of Robert Martin upon her first sighting of him in *Emma*.

27 In *Mansfield Park*, Fanny Price's parents live in relatively squalid accommodation in Portsmouth, and you can probably hear Mr Price shouting through the thin walls of the accommodation you end up sharing with Mr Martin at the end of this diversion.

28 The main storyline of this diversion is taken from *Emma*.

29 Option a) is taken from Margaret Drabble's notes to the Penguin edition of *Lady Susan / The Watsons / Sanditon* (pb ed, Penguin, London, 1974). Drabble cites William Austen-Leigh's *Memoir* and his depiction of Jane Austen's own upbringing at Steventon. Pattens were working-class footwear useful for muddy conditions. They were wooden-soled overshoes that had a flat metal circle that touched the ground, another that was nailed to the wooden sole, and metal bars between them separating the two, often by several inches (source: Wikipedia). This is why, in *Persuasion* (Volume II, chapter ii), Austen refers to 'the ceaseless clink of pattens' in Bath.

30 Lord Osborne recommends nankin (a yellowish Chinese cotton cloth) half-boots to Emma Watson in *The Watsons*.

31 Landaus and barouches were both fashionable and expensive open carriages with facing pairs of seats. The most significant difference is that while the barouche had a collapsible hood that covered the back seats when raised, the landau had two soft folding tops to cover the front and rear.

32 The idea that 'to come with a well informed mind is to come with an inability of administering to the vanity of others, which a sensible person would always wish to avoid...' is taken from *Northanger Abbey* (Volume I, chapter xiv) in which we are told, ironically, that Catherine Morland need not be ashamed of her ignorance since, 'Where people wish to attach, they should always be ignorant.'

33 Here, the heartbroken Mr Knightley flees to Antigua. This is a fleeting reference to *Mansfield Park*, in which Sir William has plantations in Antigua, where he spends a year with his eldest son Tom.

34 Captain Wentworth's fiancée, Anne Elliot, is, of course, the real heroine of *Persuasion*, from which the main storyline of this overall diversion is taken.

35 Here you are asked to take the First Impressions Test. *First Impressions* was the title Austen gave to an early version of *Pride and Prejudice*.

36 The 'hypothetical situation' you are asked to consider here is directly lifted from *Persuasion* (Volume I, chapter iv), and these are Lady Russell's views regarding the young Captain Wentworth.

ACKNOWLEDGEMENTS

❖

I would like to thank Jane Austen, very much, for being out of copyright.

I would also like to thank Louise West from Jane Austen's House and Museum for her swift and helpful responses to my questions; Sally Bayley at Balliol College, Oxford for her continuing support, infectious enthusiasm, and love of tea; Louisa Joyner and Sarah Norman at Atlantic for their hard work and patience; Sam Copeland at Robinson Literary Agency for laughing at my jokes and entertaining me with his emails when I needed it most; my Granddad, Fred, without whom I wouldn't have had the opportunity to study Austen at length; Olivia Murphy, Anna Morgan, John Lake and Robin French for their help coming up with the *Lost in Austen* title (US edition); Rachna Suri for being Rachna; and my family, especially Dad, Mark, Sue, Luke and Jodi, for all their support.

Most of all, I would like to thank my mum, Chrissie, for all her help, support and encouragement.

YOUR NOTES

❖